God's Errand Boy

Being the memoirs of
Stanley Marshall Turner
Cliff Trekker,
Railway Missionary
and
London City Missionary

inGenios
InGenios Books—ALCESTER

Cover illustration: Stanley Turner at Staithes, North Yorkshire.

Published by Ingenios Books
24 Cleeve Road,
Marlcliff, ALCESTER B50 4NR UK

God's Errand Boy
© David Turner 2016
All rights reserved
19 18 17 16   4 3 2 1
First Edition
Set in Goudy Old Style 10/14

ISBN-13: 978-1533552150
ISBN-10: 1533552150

Table of Contents

Preface by Rev. David Turner

My father made three attempts at autobiography. One was the transcript of an extended interview given to Patrick Howat, who was intending a book about the place where my father was born, a project left at Patrick's death, a follow up to his book about the branch railway. Some of the roughness is due to the attempt to compile these into one narrative. This is why a topic can occur more than once in different words. To have smoothed it out would have called for a lot of editing, and some loss of originality and liveliness. We wanted my father to speak, as unedited as possible.

Family members referred to were his brother Norman, married to Sarah, three daughters, Dorothy, Joyce, Ivy. My mother had a brother, Sidney, unmarried sister, Hilda, and May, married to George Wood.

Like his life, the book has different phases. The early chapters give a vivid account of north country childhood about the time of the first world war. Then his early Christian life and training at Cliff College, a college for Methodist lay preachers and evangelists, and a few years as a railway missionary in the Harrogate area. There were three stations, Harrogate and Knaresborough on the hills, Starbeck with its railway yards and mission hall in between. Then London life in war and peace. My mother and I travelled between London and Harrogate depending on the extent of wartime bombing in the capital. When the time came to leave Peckham, he does not say that he was feeling the rebuilding of the area imposed a strain he did not feel able to meet, but it was true.

We have included an almost unedited transcript of his Trek diary. Much of it unintelligible, but it gives the flavour.

It was very much his style that in Peckham he was known as 'Boss' not 'Sir' and that his colleagues were 'workers' not 'members'.

Old money—predecimal money was twelve pence in a shilling, twenty shillings in a pound. Could be written 1/6 (one shilling and six pence = 7½p) or £1-7-6 (one pound, seven shillings, six pence = £1.37½) or £4.10 (four pounds ten shillings = £4.50).

There are some reticences, as in all autobiographies. One omission concerns the World War 2 bomb in the mission hall. This was on two floors, the lower down steps. An incendiary came through the roof, and the warden who had a key, came down the steps, across the lower hall, up the back stairs, across the upper hall, up a long ladder into the loft and extinguished the bomb. A brave action for an uninhabited building. I have the tail cone.

The title was his own.

What higher calling could anyone have than to be errand boy to our Lord and Saviour?

Chapter 1

Beginnings

I think that our family hailed from World's End, Sowerby, Thirsk, down by the beck where there is a ford. For my second Christian name my father gave me his mother's maiden name, Marshall. I gave it to our son, David, our only child, and he gave it to his son Martin. My granddaughter, who has twins, also gave it to her son Benjamin.

Of my father's family background I know all too little. I think he was the youngest of the family; I believe there was a sister, I knew a brother—Uncle Albert who for a time lived in Thirsk and had two daughters and a son. When quite a small boy I was taken with the family to the funeral of my father's brother who had worked in the coal pit and lived in Batley where my father had lived. Uncle Ernest died from blood poison through his work. I recall sleeping either on the floor or in a drawer and seeing heavy snow with wires down and then pit men coming home black against the snow. There is a faint recall of being taken to meet my father's father on his way home—we did not go to his home.

The fact that I was named Marshall after my father's mother's maiden name leads me to think that she died while young and that perhaps my grandfather married again and that led to a rift. We never had any other contact with the Batley home. I understand that my grandma Marshall came from the Beverley side of York and think my brother tried to find the link but failed.

My father, Herbert Turner, was born in Batley among the 'dark satanic mills' of Yorkshire. It seems he was apprenticed to a blacksmith and wheelwright or millwright on leaving school but had migraine and could not continue. He was sent to the country for the good of his health, which must have been a wise decision because he lived to be 104! He moved to Sowerby, a suburb of Thirsk, at "World's End" where there was a relation, and then went to work on the land at a farm some miles away from Sowerby towards the dales.

He worked at Otterington, Tanfield and Studley Royal and it was while in this work that he seems to have met my mother Ada Suttill at the little Methodist chapel near to the farm on which he worked. He had £8 a year and his keep at his first job.

My father transferred to a better job on the North Eastern Railway and worked at Nevil Hill, Leeds and then on the Crimple-Pannal loop line and lived at Starbeck. My mother worked for Mr Johnson, a Permanent Way Inspector. Did Mr Johnson get a job for Pa? It seems their first home was in Starbeck and my earliest memory is of visiting the Johnsons where they had a big Collie named Mickie. I loved him when on Wednesdays we visited before the market visit to Knaresborough and home on the tea time train. Frequent visits were made to a neighbour in Starbeck and I was taken to a nearby hairdresser which frightened me a great deal and I was not taken again. (My father cut our hair from then on.)

My brother had had polio and had one weak leg. The story he told was that having been taken to Leeds Infirmary he and dad were stranded at Starbeck and a 'light engine' was put on to take them to Pilmoor. I can believe it was true, for Mr Johnson would be able to fix it.

Pa began on the Railway in 1900, and married in 1903. They moved to No1 Gate House, Pilmoor in 1907 and my father was second man in the platelayer gang that looked after the length from Pilmoor to the river Swale bridge beyond Brafferton Station.

He was born in 1876 so had his 100th in May 1976. Norman was born in 1905 so was five years older than me.

Speaking of early days in Starbeck my mother said 'We never saw a guinea' (21/-) as they were in a Railway house and rent was stopped.

It would seem that my mother came of a line of poor but godly country folk from near Masham in the Yorkshire dales. From poems etc. written by an uncle of my grandfather Suttill (Mother's father) It seems that a Miss Barnaby married a Suttill and had five sons. The poet was named Matthew and as my maternal Grandfather was named Matthew I take it he was named after his Uncle. I knew that the family hailed from near Masham and recall staying in a tiny cottage facing a sharp bend in the road out of Masham going north. Fearby is mentioned by the poet, and we visited High Ellington and Ellingstring. I think it was there that I saw the blacksmith at work and saw a spring for the first time. We once stayed with a cousin by the river and saw the water wheel. In Masham we visited members of my Mother's mother's family whose maiden name was Astwood, I believe. She had a brother Davy we knew well, a very little man who once took us to see him blow up a tree—he was quite a character. I recall my mother taking scissors to trim a grave in Masham church yard, much to the amusement of my father in law who was with us.

My grandfather Suttill had a sister Margaret, a delightful old lady who was very taken with our little boy David on one visit.

My mother had an older brother Joe, who lived in Thornton Watlass, married a Spence and had two daughters, Dora and Winifred, and a son Thomas. Her sister Lydia never married and younger brother George married a Bolas, and had Archibald, Hilda, Theodore, and later Edith Kezia, always known as Babs.

Grandma Suttill died of a stroke and many a time I was taken by my mother as she went to help nurse her. Two miles from Bedale to where they lived in Burrill—a long walk for a small boy. Once we got a lift in a 'trap' and I had to be lifted up. I believe Grandma Suttill's Christian name was Martha. Grandad Suttill and his wife were buried in Thornton Watlass church yard.

My mother told me she went to work at 13 for £6 per year. (Uncle Joe at 13 got £4.10.) She worked for elderly ladies and obviously learned much from them. Life must have been very hard for her. Some foods she came to dislike—one she called 'Hasty Pudding' and she told of the cake being sent into the dining room for a week, then anything left was for her use. I now see that her way of life later was coloured by these early days. All kinds of little things in the home, lay out of table, use of flowers, clean apron on Friday, the pay day, etc. all tell of early middle class training so different from her home where she said the four children did not sit for meals.

Some years ago Dorothy wrote to say they had found a book of poems which were said to be by my grandfather's uncle— The Coachman Poet, Matthew Suttill. How they knew this is not clear but I knew that Grandad Suttill hailed from the Masham area and early in life we were taken to the village mentioned in that book. It seems from the book that Matthew senior went to U. S. A. by sailing ship and he speaks of it as a land of liberty. At some time he returned by sail and steam when most of his youthful contacts had departed. It must have been a big book that Dorothy kindly based her selection on for I note page 233. Matthew must have been a godly man for his poem on The Last Supper is impressive.

THE LAST SUPPER
"Forget me not", our Saviour said
Then blest the wine, and brake the bread;
"Remember, t'was for you I died,
For you alone was crucified;
Then let those blessed emblems be
As tokens of your love to Me."
"Ah, blessed and unchanging Friend
And wilt Thou love us to the end?"

"I will and when you wait on me,
I'll set your captive spirits free".
Remember, when temptations rise,
It was for this your Saviour died.
To kill within the life of sin
And all estranged hearts to win.
I look at Christ and look again,
And look till purged of every stain.

For He's the King of saints to-day,
Who bids us ever watch and pray.
This incense He presents above,
As tokens of His constant love;
Jesus the Prophet, King and Priest,
Bids us attend this heavenly feast.
My words to you are ever new,
You shall be fed with holy dew.
    Matthew Suttill

My grandfather was named after this Matthew Suttill. He was sent to work on the land when only nine years of age and never learned to read or write. But he was a man of God and one of my early memories is hearing him pray aloud by his bed-side at night. No doubt he prayed for me and I loved him dearly.

If, as I am told, the Primitive Methodists ran a Sunday School in the waiting room at Pilmoor Station that would account for my father's link with the Thirsk Circuit of that Denomination. Before Pilmoor my parents attended the Railway Mission at Starbeck which was (and is) interdenominational and as far as I know my father had no other religious background. My mother came of Wesleyan Methodist stock and the two brothers were local preachers in the Bedale Circuit. Together my parents supported the little Primitive Methodist chapel in Little Hutton, Sessay, and he was a local preacher recognised by Thirsk for very many years.

During the First World War he went with my future father-in-law—who had the same name but was no relation—as a volunteer to France, for railway work. They'd been together before my parents moved to Pilmoor.

I know very little about Edith's family. Her father John Henry was a Starbeck man and his sisters remained in that area, one attending Starbeck Mission with her daughters. Edith's maternal grandparents lived in York, the Grandad being an engine driver living in Leman Rd. and her aunty worked in the chocolate factory.

There was an uncle living in Leeds and was at our wedding I believe. The family name was Kingan. Mother was Lucy.

Chapter 2

Pilmoor

I was born in the front bedroom of No1 The Gate House, and my mother was helped at my birth by Mrs Ireland of The Grange. I was said to have been a weak baby and mother said she spent the summer out of doors with me in 1910. Mr John H Turner of Harrogate told me that he had preached at The Grange at the monthly service connected with the Boroughbridge Wesleyan Circuit that Sunday morning, and returning to the Gate House he heard the cry of the new born Stanley. That was on June 26th: on March 26th his wife Lucy had given birth to a baby girl named Edith. Little did he know that that same 'voice' would ask his permission to marry Edith, but that is jumping 23 years.

The Harrogate Turners were close friends but not related, though Pa's work mates thought they were.

One day my mother was summoned to attend upon Lady Coates who was sitting in her carriage; there she was given a Coronation mug for my brother. Seeing the new baby in arms, there was one for me. Part of my memorabilia.

I did not go to school till I was six. That may have been due to having fits as a little child. I once sat down in a bucket of cold water. I suffered a good deal from nerves and nightmares and often made my way downstairs again before the family were ready for bed. I often stayed with the next door neighbour while Mother went to market on Wednesday. One week I had a fit and fell from top to bottom of the stairs, so that week mother took me to her old doctor at Starbeck. I just remember being examined but no medication. I suffered from chilblains and was unable to face the walk to Sessay school some winters, so that may be another reason. We lived in a very cold house.

In my early days my father became ill and could not work; how we lived I don't know but recall things were tight. My mother had me go walks with him, for I suppose she felt he would not do anything silly while I was with him, and in some way I too seemed to be looking after him. He was treated for heart trouble and later it was said to be nerves. I recall he placed great value on Dr Cassell's tablets. I suppose he had a breakdown. Perhaps it was due to this that I did not go to Sessay School until I was six.

I wonder how many double cottages there were—all alike. Picture a very large living room, entered by a big front door, no porch, and opposite that the door to the kitchen, with stairs on the right. To lessen the draught there were two folding screens covered with pictures from old magazines. Some frightened me but one I loved—a gardener father saying 'good night' to his child.

The stone floor had on it an old carpet, covered with 'clip rugs'. These were home made on a wooden frame my father had made. A large hessian sack, opened up and stretched taut, was 'prodded' with strips of old cloth. With points each five inch strip was drawn through a hole and back again through another hole. Close together they could have a pattern drawn on the hessian and light colours were for bedrooms. They were very heavy to shake. The range had a side boiler one side and oven the other, controlled by dampers. We used a lot of wood but the place was never warm in winter. One window faced east across what we called The Moor. The other faced south along the railway and the main object in view was the distant signal. Visitors teased me by asking what it was, as my reply was 'single'. Back kitchen and large larder completed the ground floor. Upstairs were two bedrooms, the rear one with sloping ceiling and low window. It had two double beds and on occasion there were three in the front room for ladies. Room in both rooms for 'floor beds'. The yard had a high wall round the pig sty, earth closet and large room with 'set pot' boiler for washing day (Monday of course). Two very big rain-water tubs and joint pump completed the picture of 'Home'. The large garden with 'hen run', hen house and shed was the limit of our domain, though there was an unofficial opening at the rear, so that we could let the hens out if the farmer gave permission after harvest. We 'gleaned'—potatoes, etc. — by permission. There was no way out to the road.

While there was a large cast iron warning plate north of the road; it was clear that the original architect expected railway people to be excepted from the possible forty shilling fine, because the right of way from No1 dwelling to the public road was by use of the 'line-side'. It may be seen from the photograph mentioned, the nearest rail was about eighteen feet from the garden gate. In fact it was not possible to go to school or church or anywhere east of the track without crossing it without any guard whatever. The result was that we grew up to look upon the railway as part of our domain, part of our playground.

This was not the case with what we called the Company's Cottages, but I believe their front garden gates opened onto the line-side of the main line and children making their way to the road bridge walked along an unguarded pathway. Yet I never remember a child being hurt, or having a narrow escape—we were 'train-wise'. No doubt some ran across the crossing on their way to Sunday School and we wheeled coals across it when old enough.

Our clothes posts were along the line side, and we had a garden by the Moor siding gate until a visiting guard (?) harvested the potato crop and stuck the tops back in!

The First World War

I was four when war broke out and it must have coloured my early days. My earliest memory of my mother was her singing about the home. They had attended the Railway Mission and were familiar with the Sankey book. I can still remember her singing:

I shall know Him, I shall know Him,
 —by the print of the nails in His hands.
and
There is sunshine in my soul today
More glorious and bright
Than glows in any earthly sky;
For Jesus is my light.

But I do not remember her singing about the home after the war began.

One faint memory is of her sitting in the train at Pilmoor station looking at the paper (Leeds Mercury I suppose). I could not read but recall columns of black print. I have had to check that this was real, it seems there were pages of deaths in the newspapers of the time.

Two elderly ladies had kept the gates at Pilmoor and had then moved to York where my people visited them. On one occasion my mother took me there and I recall her taking me to see a bombed house near the home of the Wrights. It was in York station that another memory stuck tight. We were sitting in the compartment when a young soldier dashed in and through, leaving the door on to the track wide open. My father quickly closed it and when a Red Cap (Policeman) came, he sat back as though nothing had happened but the man was followed and taken prisoner. I asked what would happen to him and we all felt sorry for him but I was not told. I think that even then I knew the men were shot for desertion on the battlefield.

The family visited my Great Uncle John who had been in the Indian army, a big man. He and his wife had had the care of the Workhouse, but at that time were in charge of the Thirsk Isolation hospital. Wounded soldiers were there dressed in blue and as a small boy I went to see them, I must have been about six or seven. They dressed me up and wrapped puttees round my legs from ankle to thigh. Soldiers wore them but I could not bend my knee. It was fun for them and I did not mind—I suppose I liked to 'show off'.

I recall that we were warned not to pick up and eat sweets. It was said the "Enemy" were dropping them to poison children, such was the atmosphere of war. From time to time we heard loud explosions and one very big one when a factory blew up many miles away. We always knew about these, for the pheasants called very loudly.

My Mother made all my clothes until I was quite a big lad and as Khaki cloth was available—castoffs. I wore shorts made of it and, I think, a coat. I wore a balaclava in winter and called it a hemlet (another problem word).

There came the day when my father left for France; he and Mr John Turner and others had volunteered to do six months railway work there. I recall seeing him off and walking back up the line (our usual way home) and bursting into tears. My brother beat me for it as no doubt he did not want my mother to be upset. I don't know the date (1917) of this event but it began a difficult period for us as when the men returned from France they were sent to work at Gateshead. Mother had to face life without her partner for long periods (two years) and to see a young man take my father's place on the 'length' as it was called. Those must have been difficult days for my mother, but it opened my eyes to another world as we visited Gateshead and saw barefoot children begging for bread from men going on shift. I did not understand a word of the local dialect. I recall that mother was shocked when the women began to wear men's trousers as they cut pit props on the moor.

One small incident was that a man we did not like who had found us picking flowers in a wood he was responsible for, agreed that mother could have a fallen tree 'if she could get it'. It had fallen partly into the old brick pond near our home and was very difficult to get. However she and Norman, with what help I could give, cut it up and brought it home for fire-wood. Dad was not home for Christmas and mother hoped he would get; Norman and I and the other Turner children came downstairs very early to get our 'stockings', stood on the fire irons and woke the household. The parting went on for two years and both families must have had a hard time.

Sweets were not available during the war as far as I know and we made do with Locust beans—an odd taste—and liquorice sticks. Later there were black (liquorice) laces on sale. Later still there were machines on stations where a very thin bar of chocolate was passed out for the insertion of a penny. We did not use them as that was our weekly pocket money for many years.

Late in the war or after it, we had war games. A soldier friend came to stay and dug us a trench and we filled old tin cans with sand for grenades. (No one got killed in these games)

At some time we were let out of school to see an Aeroplane! Eventually they became quite common as they followed the main railway line north and south as navigational aids! There was also what was called the aerodrome—a big field on the hillside near Helperby on the Boroughbridge roadside. A small hut remained for many years. From this planes flew and crashed. One near The Hall and another came down safely near The Grange. For years Pa had a bit of the broken propeller at home.

I still have the Christmas card my father sent from France—lace work. We were afraid of air raids and dreaded the glow from Middlesborough furnaces that lit up the sky some nights, miles and miles away though they were. We saw too on occasion the play of the Northern Lights in the northern sky. Another war memory is of the canes we were proud to have with regimental 'head' in 'silver' colour. We also collected Cap badges and later Cigarette cards.

There was a well down the garden, and another between the two cottages, with a pump each side of the wall. There was a wooden bung to put in the spout so that the other house could draw water. When the local authority put in piped water, they took the handles off the pumps. The well down the garden was eventually covered with wood, and soil on top. When the house was sold after my niece Dorothy died, I wrote to the new owner to tell him about this well, as it could be a danger.

My parents were marvellously hospitable. For example, at the Sunday School Anniversary people came from Harrogate; they included the other Turner family, and their children Edith, Hilda and Sydney. (Another child came later.) Eventually I married their daughter. In the house we had two or three double beds in our front bedroom. The females occupied that and the males occupied two double beds in the back room, and with beds also on the floor. My mother could entertain more than a dozen people. The other Turner family would also all come for Christmas. There was also a widow whom my parents befriended and she came for holidays. I fell in love with her fourteen-year-old daughter. It was calf love and didn't last. I found out there was another boy and I could have killed him!

It was always amusing to me and I always used to say that if there was anybody in need, anyone begging, they didn't go to N°2, nearest the road. There was some psychology working and they thought that everybody would go to the house nearest the crossing, so they always went to N°1, the second house.

We went on holiday once a year. We always went to Staithes and I was taken there as a baby. We stayed with a Miss Lizzie Unthank, who was deaf and had lost two brothers at sea in a coble. She was a lovely saintly soul. When we got there we always slipped into their dialect, otherwise she would not have been able to read our lips. As quite a small child I had my normal North Yorkshire accent at home but when I got to 'Steerthes' I spoke like Staithes people and I used their phraseology and their intonation, and she could understand. On one occasion Miss Unthank took us to a home where there was a deaf and dumb lady; she wasn't in sight when we arrived there but Miss Unthank picked up a brush and rapped it against the stairs and the deaf and dumb lady came running down the stairs—she'd felt the vibrations.

We were like part of the railway company at Pilmoor. We walked each way along the line, depending on where we were going. We went to the station that way but visitors had to be taken to the bridge and then walked along the cinder path beside the main line. Looking back it was an amazing community, albeit quite absurd in some ways. We took it as though the railway belonged to us. My father bought disused sleepers, at a shilling each. Some of them must have been in good condition because the hen house and the shed next door were all made of sleepers.

Living at Pilmoor

My mother always said that the local property belonged to the Christian Faith Society. The triangle between the road and Pilmoor station had never been cultivated from ancient history, except the field quite near to the station and the station house, which was cultivated by Ox Close Farm. Ox Close had a gate across the railway from its fields on the east of the main line to this small field on the west. Eventually one of the

Potters took it over. Next to the field there was a row of trees and the rest of it was CFS.

If you dug down to any depth at Pilmoor you got to what my father called 'mowpan'. It wasn't mud or heavy soil. The Moor, which had never been cultivated, was quite fascinating to me. It included the area near the Moor cottages and towards the station and the two brick ponds. It went up to a gate that led to the Grange. It wasn't up to the main line side, at The Wink, which is what we called the cottages. At the Wink there was a deposit of silver sand; they were never sure whether they could make glass from it, but there wasn't enough of it and so they didn't. The area was never fenced in my day. The brick ponds were very deep and dangerous and we were warned that we must never go there. It wasn't until we were in our early teens that we went to get wild birds eggs there, which my mother always welcomed. We knew how to drop them in water to see how fertile they were. Another thing was that if you held a needle suspended from cotton over an egg it goes lengthways or round and round. That is to do with the sex of the chick.

My parents—and as I look back it was very funny—were strictly tee-total but occasionally Clare Topham, the game-keeper for the Coates family, would come and my mother would give him some rhubarb wine. (Clare Topham's son was also called Clare and another son eventually became keeper.)They lived in the keeper's cottage near the entrance to Pilmoor Hall. Later Clare Topham became the Coates's head keeper, after a Mr Rayner, and he left the keeper's cottage. It was Sir Edward Coates at first when I was a child, then it was Sir Clive. Once a year we were allowed into the gardens at Helperby Hall; they were beautifully kept. Eventually it became all derelict, which was very sad.

The men of Pilmoor were always very friendly towards youngsters. The area where they lived, at the lineside cottages, we called The Wink. Although the people weren't necessarily churchgoing, it was a very God-fearing group, in the sense that they were upright, honest, straightforward people. I never remember anyone getting into trouble. The policeman came occasionally and I used to hide—but what in the world I had a guilty conscience about I don't know. Having said that, we did do a bit of poaching. There was only one man that I know of who was ever known to get drunk. Mrs Topham used to say that he fell off, when he cycled from Helperby; there was a little rise before you got to the keeper's cottage and he couldn't make it, and that's where he fell off.

The Greaves family lived at Ox Close. (The cottage by the Sessay road at the entrance to their farm was the home of the Headmaster of Sessay school, Mr Richardson.) Mr Greaves died quite young and the Coates family took pity on Mrs Greaves and allowed her to go into the keeper's cottage, which after the Tophams had moved out had become nearly derelict. She brought up her family there. There was Harold, Alan and Nina. Dorothy, my niece, kept in touch with Alan Greaves because of his bringing flowers for the grave in Sessay church- yard. He went to live in Darlington. When war broke out I got a letter from Harold Greaves to say that he'd been out of work but he'd had training as a bricklayer, and asking whether there was any possibility of work in London. I knew the local builder in Peckham; they were just building street shelters. So I went to the builder and asked him if he could give a friend of mine a job. He agreed, and so Harold came and stayed with us, and he found his wife in our church; my wife made the wedding dress for his bride. He stayed right through the War and the bombing; we slept in the shelter. There were four of us, men, eventually in the shelter. They had two sons, who became doctors.

There were two old brick cottages on the Moor. The Martins lived in the first house, nearest us; before them it was the Lancasters. When I was about four I was allowed to go though our gates and walk along the verge to go to see Annie Lancaster, to play. That was when, as a very young child, I first appreciated another personality—she had a will of her own and she wanted to play her way. The Lancasters must have moved very early, because I don't remember her much after my early childhood. One day when I was at school there came a message: Maurice Martin's father had died suddenly. The mistress called me out to go home with him. I didn't go all the way home with him but came to the lane end, where there was a post box on the corner, trying to persuade him that his father was all right after all, but he wasn't. Mrs Martin had her shop on the Moor. I remember her very well, although I can't remember anything much about the shop. She was very nice though.

The Cravens lived in the second house on the Moor, the one nearest to the railway. It was quite a big family, with three sons and a daughter. The father was called Mark and the eldest son was also called Mark, who was the more gentlemanly type of the family. Then there was Holmes, who for some reason was known as 'Tabs' but presumably was fond of cigarettes, Woodbines, which cost tuppence a packet and even in those days were called 'coffin nails'. I've always felt guilty about that: for some reason two of us raised tuppence and went to the shop in Sessay to get a packet of Woodbines. I had to tell several lies to get them because the shopkeeper said to me, "Your father doesn't smoke." I said "Oh yes he does" and it was a lie! Then there was Frank Craven, who was the youngest. I think that the daughter had gone into service before my day. The big pond holes were just before their garden.

My earliest recollection of the gatehouse next to us is of the two Miss Wrights, who later moved to York. They kept in touch and my mother took me to see them. This was during the first World War and my mother also took me to see a bombed house in York. After them there was Tom Wells, and his wife who was the gatekeeper, and they had no children. They were very kind to me. In their day the little cabin at the crossing was always kept closed but it was kept in spotless condition. It used to fill with flies. The gate had a lock on it which didn't always work. Across the road there was a signal—a board signal. Just once, when I was an older boy, a driver pulled up because the board was against him. I ran across the road and switched it round and he went on his way. The Beilbys lived there later and Mr Beilby worked on the railway. It was very sad because one or two families who came to the gatehouse lost the husbands.

There was a not-very-nice woodman on the estate with whom we quarrelled because he caught us in Spring Wood collecting lillies-of-the-valley; he swore at my mother, which I never forgave him for. The same individual had the threshing machine, a Massey Harris, and when I was old enough I went to help, to get a day's work. They put me on what they called 'cutting bands', which were the pieces of string round the sheaves. I had to climb onto the threshing machine, cut a band and hand it to him. Eventually they forked up some very weedy stuff, full of thistles and all the rest. I couldn't find the band and this fellow swore at me. I stopped the job—I leaned over the side and called for the foreman—and refused to work any more. It was the only time I ever went on strike!

The Railway

The gang that looked after the line consisted of Tom Wells, the ganger, my father, and the third man whose name I can't remember. They had to slash the hedges and mow the grass beside the track. In summer they had to weed the track which was yellow all over with Stonecrop. They weeded it by hoeing, all the way to Brafferton. If it rained they went into a cabin, which was of course made of sleepers, and they played Merrills, or Nine Men's Morris. They had made their own; they'd burnt the holes and they made their own little wooden pegs, some with holes in hollowed out and the others plain. With this game you have nine holes, then inside nine holes, then inside another nine holes; the idea was to complete a row, when your opponent could take one off you if he completed a row. My father was an absolute expert and he used to make what he called a Running Jill, but what in the world that was I didn't know. They had to complete a three and, having completed a three, they had to work through to the next one and complete another one.

The passing trains, as many as five on Saturday, must have been a constant cause of concern, for when the train was due mother would call me and say "shut the garden gate". I did not then understand that with me, a small boy, behind it I was safe—somehow it was linked to the train passing!

Within sight of our home was what was known as a distant signal usually set at danger, as the next one was at the Station half a mile from my home. It was hard for me to say 'signal', so I was often teased to try it and it came out 'single'.

As a little boy of four or five my father sometimes took me with him. Normally I just played out, and pushed their bogie about. There was one particular platelayers' cabin about halfway between the gatehouse and Brafferton. I have a faint recollection that, looking through a hole in the cabin wall, they could see the Inspector walking along the line from Brafferton. I was poked over the hedge and told to hide until he'd gone.

Perhaps because my father spent his life maintaining that line to Brafferton, we looked upon the railway as ours and we walked along it for our Sunday walk as far as Spring Wood and back.

The railway had a siding on the Moor and before my day the railway had run across the road to the brickyard. We played in the siding. There were two lines and we pushed the trucks around: we pushed them down, over the points, changed the points and then back into the other line. They were heavy but we got them going by levering them with a bit of wood, either under the wheel or through the spokes— terribly dangerous!

A lot of the railwaymen of Pilmoor had had First Aid training. There was a strange accident and it reflects upon the local railwaymen to their credit. There came an occasion when what was called a 'stationary engine' was sited in that siding on the Moor. It had a circular saw and it was alongside one of the lines, cutting timber. I was told that a man, very foolishly, sat astride the saw to sharpen it, but without taking the belt off first. The not very clear-witted engine attendant wanted to fill his boiler with water and he started the engine. He cut this man's leg very badly. They got in touch with the station and the railwaymen came down and saved his life. Thirsk was the nearest ambulance station and if they hadn't had the First Aid training he probably would have died.

An engine driver that I remember as a small boy always had a smiling face. Often he would drop off a little toy as he went by. One thing they did, which I am sure was against the rules, was to kick off lumps of coal. My mother told me that this was Mr Joe Dickinson and when I eventually became railway missionary at Starbeck, Joe Dickinson had retired and he was the one who paid me my week's money.

There was an incident after I left Pilmoor. An excursion had come late one Saturday night and the engine ran round the coaches and was ready to set off along the branch to Brafferton and Harrogate. The driver, instead of backing far enough to allow the signalman to put the points across, was still on the line that went to the chock end. Being a Saturday night and on his last trip he was in a hurry to get home; he really opened up and went as fast as he could into the chock end. The people were very badly shaken and my parents took them in. My brother took some of them by car to Helperby.

Dick Potter was on duty at the gates at Starbeck once. He told us how he looked up and he saw this huge diesel coming down towards him. He slammed the gates shut. There was a lorry driver and he looked up and swore at Dick because he'd put the gates in front of him. Then he saw this engine come slowly through and he went as white as a sheet. It went half way to York before they stopped it.

Sundays

For us and for many other families at that time, Sundays had to be a completely different day. My mother's approach to Sunday was that she would put the oven on, which was originally a side oven. She would take the damper out so that the heat went into the oven, she would put the dinner in, but she wouldn't make a cake because that would have been unnecessary work. Whenever I went to my grandfather's at Burrill, near Bedale, we weren't allowed to read anything but the Bible or perhaps the Christian Herald which had little drawings of events at the top of the page. A Missionary being attacked by a lion etc. as, of course, photos were not used. Looking at it from today you might say we were very restricted but we weren't. Sunday was a happy day; it was a day that was completely different. We were at ease; there was no friction; there was nothing to disturb us. It was a wonderful day and I don't look back on it with any regret at all.

At Pilmoor as a family we had the Wesleyan Sunday School class in the morning, the Primitive Methodist service in the afternoon and the Anglican service in the evening. We, my brother and I, rarely complained about going to church so often on Sundays and I always said that this prepared me for my life's work, which was always interdenominational.

John Wesley started Methodism, but early on they divided into the Wesleyan Methodists and the Primitive Methodists; I don't know why. The Primitives were started by a man called Thomas Clowes who was a more outgoing, evangelical type; this was after Wesley's death. They ran a lot of open air meetings that were called 'camp meetings', whereas the Wesleyans went a little bit towards the Church of England—they were a little more orderly. The Primitives were very strongly evangelical; their services were a bit more informal and in the early days there was a lot of shouting and a fair amount of excitement. They were known as 'ranters'. At one point in his own life John Wesley said "I became more vile" and he began to preach in the open air. He had huge meetings and he transformed Cornwall. The Primitives came in with the Wesleyans at the time of the Union, in 1931, I think.

My parents told me that the Sunday School had begun in the waiting room at Pilmoor station. Then I imagine it was switched to the Irelands' at Pilmoor Grange; Matt Ireland and his wife ran the Sunday School at their home there. They must have been Wesleyans, for an adult service was held there under the Boroughbridge Wesleyan Methodist Circuit each month. Matt Ireland was the foreman for Mr Driffield at Pilmoor Grange. Pilmoor Grange was a very interesting building, because you went in the back door into a huge kitchen and you went through into what I assume was the dining room. That was all laid out with benches. One of my very earliest recollections is of when I was a very tiny boy sitting on these backless benches and dangling my feet because I couldn't touch the floor. Matt Ireland, Mark Craven and my father were the three teachers. The Irelands later moved to, I believe, Crake. They had a son called Alfie.

After the Irelands left, my father took charge of the Sunday School, which was transferred from The Grange to our house at 1 Pilmoor Gatehouse. My father ran it for many, many years. Strictly speaking the Sunday School at Pilmoor was part of the Wesleyan Boroughbridge circuit. I am sure that the Irelands were Wesleyan but I suppose that it might have been Primitive early on. At the Sunday School we sang a hymn and had a scripture reading. My mother had a good voice and my brother eventually played the organ. Mark Craven or Pa would speak. He was a shepherd before he came to work at The Grange and he was nearly illiterate. He was a patient man and a lovely character. He would tell us stories and very largely he got them from the Christian Herald, which was probably the only thing he ever read.

For the music there was a harmonium to start with, without stops. That was later put to the side and used as a side table and a more up-to-date American organ came, which my brother played. I don't think he played particularly well but he played. I am sure that my father will have bought that himself, rather than its being provided by the Methodist chapel.

We had a collection and the money that came in was very much spent on the children. We had an annual outing by train to Redcar. I well remember that as we went by the side of a river, before we got to the sea or anywhere near Redcar, Frank Craven cried out "My, what a lot of water!" He had never seen so much water. He had never seen the sea and he must have been quite a big boy, of 11 or 12, so what he thought when he saw that I don't know.

Dick Potter made a very kind comment about my parents and the Sunday School. He said that when he looked back he realised how interested they were in what they called 'us kids', which was a very nice tribute to their interest in him and other youngsters.

After Sunday School there would be a walk while dinner was prepared. What my mother jokingly called "Set Tom Set" took place. My Father would 'set' Mr Craven. Walking nearly to his home they turned and came back nearly to ours and so on until dinner. Afternoon involved a three mile walk or later cycle to Sessay Primitive Methodist Chapel at Little Hutton. As a small child I was taken in a push chair and eventually I would be taken on the crossbar of a bike but sometimes we walked. My mother never cycled—she walked. It was almost out of Sessay as no doubt the Church would oppose the building of a chapel. My father often took the service as he was on "the plan" of the Thirsk Circuit. (It was by this Circuit that I was given a letter authorising me to read the lesson at services later in life.) I think we stayed for tea with a blind lady in early days, or was it for special occasions. Later there was just the afternoon service. I still recall a blind lady giving out a hymn; either "I'll praise my Maker" or "A charge to keep I have" and at the Love Feast there were testimonies. A special was a "Camp Meeting" peculiar to the P.M.s or the "Ranters" as the P.M.s were disparagingly called. This was an Open Air evangelistic meeting. When free of the Sessay meeting we attended the little church in Pilmoor and became friendly with the Brafferton Curate. Our home was always a point of call for the clergy. No doubt God was preparing me for work in an interdenominational Society.

I don't know when my father became a Primitive Methodist. In the Thirsk circuit there was a chapel at Borrowby, on the other side of Thirsk, and another at Little Hutton. Little Hutton chapel had been built onto the roadside in a most peculiar fashion, on the end of a house. There was just a footpath between it and the road. It was out of line with the rest of the property.

My parents never tried to instil religion into us; they expected us to fit in. Pa taught us in Sunday School and both of them just lived sincere Christian lives. My mother particularly influenced me for good. I rather feared my Father as he could apply the belt on occasion and early in my life he had a 'short fuse', but how graciously he mellowed later.

The vicar of Sessay was a Payne-Gallwey. He was related to the Payne-Gallweys of Pilmoor. He was pretty remote and had a huge vicarage at Sessay. The chimneys stood up huge above the rest of the house. This is because the top storey of the house caught fire and was burned out. I saw it on fire as I cycled home from work in Thirsk. So they eventually reduced the house by one storey but left the chimneys standing.

At Pilmoor, and for the people living there, the Sunday School Anniversary was the occasion of the year. It was in Mr Ireland's barn then, after he moved to Crayke, Mr Pick's barn, then Mr White's barn. I think Mr Pick was very happy to have it there, but as far as I could gather Mr White wasn't that interested. However, he had to go on letting us use his barn as he'd have earned a very bad name indeed if he hadn't. Mr White had been in Canada and he was a go-getter.

The men of the hamlet, Pilmoor, co-operated absolutely on the Sunday School Anniversary, whether they ever went to church themselves or not. If there wasn't grain in the barn they would clean it and they filled sacks and put benches on them for the congregation to sit. They would go to near the cottages where there was the silver sand, and fill the bags with silver sand. They would then put the bags down in the barn and the planks across the tops. They took the barn doors off to form the platform.

For some weeks before the Anniversary we were taught new songs. That was an annual thing that had to be done. That took quite a time, as did learning the recitations. The recitations were not long—perhaps four lines—and we always had a funny one. They, and the songs, were specially written for children's Sunday School anniversaries. I used to race through mine because my memory wasn't very good. One title that I remember was "I reckon we'll pull froo." I didn't say that one but in broad Yorkshire it must have been marvellous. Another was "When father's worn his trousers out they passed to brother John, then Mother turns them inside out and Willy puts them on." It was absolute doggerel but it raised a laugh.

Pilmoor Church and Reading Room

The individual who was responsible for the idea of the Reading Room was called Richards, I think. He had been an officer in the First World War. I imagine that he would officially open it. I was a small boy and my parents were told that if we subscribed five shillings we could have a brick with our initials on it. My brother and I had bantams, and my parents said "well, if you want a brick you must sell your bantam." I wept bucketfuls. The bantam went and the brick was paid for, and I've still got it. My niece Dorothy found them when it was demolished. The Reading Room was used for billiards—I learned to play it there.

The Anglican service was at Pilmoor church and I went practically every Sunday night. Mr McNeile was the Anglican vicar of Brafferton, but we didn't often see him and it was his curate who came to Pilmoor. One curate was called Holmes, I think. My mother told me that Pilmoor church was known as a Chapel of Ease; it was a daughter church. We never had communion there. My parents were such that the curate would come to our home far more freely than perhaps he went to any other home at Pilmoor. He was always welcome and there was never any feeling between us that we were Methodist and he was Church of England. He was like a big brother and on a summer evening Norman and I would walk with him when he left us, perhaps to the keeper's cottage; it was called 'setting'—it was setting him on his way, really.

In Pilmoor church there was a beautiful big organ, like a glorified American one, really. It wasn't a pipe organ but a reed organ. It was huge. We were brought up to have tremendous respect for the church, more particularly the Church of England than the Free church. I planned to climb the highest tree that I could find, but not the trees within the iron railings that surrounded the little church. The church was a typical little Anglican building, rectangular with a very small entrance porch and what must have been a very tiny vestry though I was never in it. Pews right and left of the centre aisle and then the area from where the preacher officiated and the pulpit. I never minded going with my mother on a Sunday evening, and one or two amusing things happened. We had a curate who was a bit absent minded and we could see that he was searching his surplice and pockets as the service went on and then he said 'There will be no sermon this evening'—I think we had a hymn and then he said 'There will be a sermon after all. ' He'd found it! We had the very happiest relationship with all concerned. I can't remember who it was that cleaned it, cleaned the building and attended the evensong, but I think at one time Alice Wallbank would be the organist. Had the birds needed a sanctuary, there was one within those iron railings—ivy for the sparrows, the roof for the jackdaws and of course the trees; not that they needed any shelter from the crowds in the middle of a moorland area.

One very interesting point was that the gate didn't quite fit the iron post and over the years one of the members of the tit family entered through the bolt hole into the hollow iron post and reared a nestful of young, over quite a number of years.

On a cloudy, stormy afternoon a mizzlethrush or stormcock would take up his position on the top of the highest point and pour out song which could be heard over quite a distance.

The church was a focal point, a reminder of spiritual things in the middle of what at one time must have been a very busy little community, when there were two diggings for clay for the brickworks, one for the ponds near the main line and one very near indeed to the branch line, but perhaps that will crop up somewhere else. I may have written elsewhere that the reading room was used for whist drives and from time to time they would arrange all the details including borrowing table tops and trestles from my father so that they could put on a tea. We did not have much to do with that side of things for we did not agree with the playing of cards or anything to do with gambling. That was one of the things that must have sort of set us aside a little bit from the rest of the community. Whether we were any better or not I leave that to others.

I was very fond of my Grandfather Suttill and he was very kind to me. When I was old enough I would cycle to stay with him in the school holiday and often he would greet me with, "Oh I thout thou would come today." I wondered how often he was disappointed. I slept in one room and could hear him praying aloud in the next room each night. He had gone to plough when he was eight and could not read or write but was a keen Christian. I know he had a very great dislike of playing cards and called them the Devil's Playthings, which led me to think he might have gambled in his youth. (Edith seemed to have noted this for she too hated them and year by year put packs in the fire in holiday homes.) When in Burrill I was taken to help with garden work and no doubt learned a great deal. I had to work hard while there and was sent down to a a field called the Penny Ting to collect his two or three cows for milking. My mother told how she worked as a girl in the harvest field 'Making bands'—that was twisting straw to bind the sheaf.

We went to the chapel in the village on Sunday and I recall one old gent who always prayed very quickly using the same phrase 'I would not rush like an unthinking hoss into battle.' However I was impressed with the 'Love Feast' held each year. A glass of water was passed round and a large biscuit given. There were testimonies and a sermon. I was once taken up the dale to Gunnerside for a huge gathering for such a Love Feast.

Aunty Lydia was housekeeper to Grandad for many years and they were both most kind to me and made Edith very welcome when I began to take her there, years later.

My grandfather would never dig on Good Friday as our Lord's blood was shed on the ground that day. However that did not mean a day off—we had to help to shift manure from the midden up to the field at the back of the house. I was like a donkey pulling the wheel barrow. Then once I recall we were to teach a young bull to be led by a halter as each cow had been trained. The process was for one to pull and the other to push the rear end until the animal gave in and did as it was taught. It was quite a job and it was well I was a strong boy.

'Royal Oak' day, which I think was the 29th of May, was when we sang out "Royal Oak Day if you don't give us holiday, we'll all run away." On that day we chased the girls with nettles if they did not hold a sprig of Oak! Another nearby was Empire Day when we had flag papers showing red on the map, that was the 24th. One was a holiday I believe.

Games

Football, if we had one, on the Rectory field, or with a small ball in the playground. Cricket wherever we could find a level pitch, home-made bat or the result of a birthday. 'Last across', a general chase game played on the grass triangle formed by roads outside the school. The last one had to seek to catch one to take their place. At the appropriate season of the year out came our 'whip and tops'. Who decided the time for these and other seasonal games is a mystery. Marbles came and went. Each boy had a 'hoop' even if it was just off a barrel. Ours were iron for Pa could fashion iron, and with them a long piece with a hook on the end. It made a long trek more attractive, though I do not recall that we took them on the two miles to school.

Only girls did skipping or played shuttle cock. We played some kind of rounders and when small did the usual playground games. 'The farmers in his den', 'In and out the window', pulling games and leapfrog. In season much time was spent 'bird nesting' for we had collections and thought little of taking eggs on a limited scale. Eggs of waterhens and game birds could be used for food and we knew now to decide if a waterhen's eggs were good for use by placing them in water but I cannot remember how. One egg mystery I have never solved—I recall my parents taking a needle on cotton and holding it over hens (chickens) eggs. Each egg either made the needle turn in circles or from end to end but if this was to show fertility or more likely sex I don't know (but it still works!). A local joke about bird nesting—Vicar to small boy who had collected eggs (and did what we often did) placed eggs in cap. 'You don't rob nests do you my boy'—'Oh no, Sir. ' Vicar to small boy, 'Good boy,' patting boy on head. Result— a mess.

Some time was spent with our pets. I had a grey doe and Norman a white buck. With them I learned some facts of life. Parents never mentioned sex and we learned from older children the 'unbelievable' fact that humans did what we were familiar with animals doing.

Our three legged pussy slept in what we called the Copper House where the 'set pot' was for laundry. One day I heard her calling and she was giving birth to kittens. One very early pet was a bantam. Norman had an owl, a very smelly bird and one that slit his thumb before it went. Like all young folk we collected—for us 'Cig' cards. Winter evenings found us limited to oil lamp and candles. As a small boy I played trains with bricks and had little difficulty in amusing myself. Later I read a great deal but often had to give up and lie down with sick headache. Years later I was told I had astigmatism, but school did not find that out.

One very dangerous pastime was for us boys to get together and play with wagons on the nearby siding. How we escaped injury I don't know. Another, less dangerous, venture was to get near the top of the highest tree in our area. I still remember passing swiftly down and coming to my senses on my back below. I was alone as usual. My father gave us each a whistle and we knew we could call for help. When his railway whistle went we knew to hasten home. I still have the one he gave me.

Rabbit catching provided good sport at harvest time. As the horse-drawn binder (in early days) went round and round, the time came for rabbits in the middle to make a run for their lives. Most did get away unless some man had a gun. Apart from this, a more serious attempt was made to snare or trap rabbits for food. Nothing was wasted for the dry skin was sold for a penny.

Rabbits make me think of food and they played a big place in our provision. Mother was well able to skin and cut up the animal into approved parts. Rabbit pie was welcome; done in the side oven in the living room, until an elderly lady they befriended, Miss Hutton from Thirsk—who had stomach ache at the thought of the train journey from Thirsk through Sessay to Pilmoor when coming on holiday—bought us a paraffin stove. An alternative was for the rabbit being put through the hand mincer and flavoured with mace, it formed an attractive paste, known as 'potted' rabbit.

Mother went by train to market on Wednesdays and brought home extra items in addition to groceries brought monthly by my Uncle. He would deliver a ten stone sack of flour, and other bulk items. One treat was when a sheep's head came. It was boiled with nettles to flavour it and made a welcome broth. Another treat was when sprats were brought and fried. Eventually we had tomatoes known as Bachelor's Buttons. The 'Fish Man' called weekly, and the butcher, so we were well supplied if money was available, otherwise we went without such extras. The garden kept us in vegetables and for the winter potatoes, carrots and beet went into a clamp we called a pie—a heap of vegetables, straw, then earth over all and frost free. I recall that most visitors went home with a cabbage or other gift and railway men from town often took home a rabbit. We gave little thought to killing—it was a means to an end and there was no needless cruelty, though the time came when traps were forbidden, but that was after my country days.

In early days a pig was kept, the property had a pigsty built in the end of the yard, and I recall the killing by a visiting butcher. In the living room there were two rows of hooks from the ceiling to take hams and sides. I'm afraid I don't remember ham being served, so perhaps they were sold. Breakfast often comprised very fat thin belly bacon fried with onions and then the gravy thickened, cheap and tasty for a winter morning. We did have a cereal named FORCE, I believe.

If a pheasant hit the telephone wire, Pa would bring it home for a treat and as we kept hens (chickens) we had the occasional fowl.

A rather sick joke of my father puzzled me for some time. Mother needed dentures and went to York for them. On her return my father said "She's got t'pig in her mouth." Evidently the pig had been sold to pay for the treatment.

For puddings, suet dumplings with gravy or suet pudding with white sweetened sauce was served. Steamed puddings—one named Aunty Margaret's had jam put in the bottom of the basin before the whole was steamed so on being served it had a jam top. Rice pudding was put in the side oven and mother said it must "CREE"; a long cook produced a good pudding.

Yorkshire pudding was a must, the idea being that it filled, but we loved it. My grandfather had his with milk and sugar. Some put apple in it.

I took a packed lunch to school and came to dislike sandwiches. Cold beef from a cheap roast was often discarded. One good thing I liked was a date pasty, I think there was a pump at school for drinking water. The occasional egg called for us to have lots of bread with it, a habit that has remained. For special occasions my mother would buy a tongue, pickle it and put it in a earthenware pot with a weight on top; the weight being a few inches of railway line, used as a door stop in the yard as a rule. Sago pudding, apple pie and all kinds of cakes made up the traditional Yorkshire tea. When I came south and saw what was provided for tea it was a bit of a shock. Christmas cake making was a fine art and mother would take delight in tasting as many Christmas cake gifts as possible. Visitors had Christmas cake and Wensleydale cheese and ginger wine. But some had something stronger. Though my parents were life long teetotallers, mother did make rhubarb or other wine. She did not appear to class it as alcoholic. I recall the local keeper saying, "My that was a drop of good." From time to time we heard a bang and a cork had blown off a bottle of wine. Home made medicines were prepared—brimstone and treacle for one, and a bad cold mixture of honey, vinegar and possibly lemon. Veno lightening cough cure, Sloanes liniment for Pa's back which burned my hand if I was asked to apply it, were among simple remedies used. Doctor was very rarely consulted. One memory of the local Doctor was his giving me a lift in his motor car, an open two seater, my first ride.

We usually wore heavy boots which were treated with dubbin. Pa was kept busy putting new soles on, or renewing toe or heel 'plates'. Hob nailed boots were the usual farm worker's protection for the feet. I suffered a good deal from chilblains and had to be off school sometimes through them. They were treated with Snowfire but there was a saying that the contents of the chamber pot (in common use) worked wonders. I cannot remember trying it. Shorts gave little protection from the cold and only older boys had knee breeches and leggings. A Staithes type 'jersey' with the rope pattern and a white stiff collar completed our attire. I did not have a bought pair of trousers until eleven or twelve I believe and being cheap they were soon well up my legs after getting them wet.

I never had skates but we enjoyed slides on the ice and we had a sledge but no hills. When a bit older we went to the Beck in Summer and us younger boys did not have bathing costumes. Only passing trains had a view of us so it did not matter. I did not learn to swim as the beck was shallow and the local river too dangerous. There was a story that my father saved a man's life at Brafferton from the river Swale, so we were forbidden to try a dip there.

We made the most of seasonal fruit etc., growing gooseberries, black currants, apples, strawberries, red currants, and marrows—all being made into jam along with brambles, as we called blackberries or 'Blegs' as the Geordies called them. On occasion I would collect crab apples for jelly and from the same field we collected mushrooms in season. We did not ask permission: it was taken for granted that we could go there. Mother was good at collecting blackberries and when the moor had been visited by people from town as was often the case, she could go and get what she needed. She used to say they trample bushes down and if you look underneath there you will find good fruit.

Apples were stored under the beds in the back bedroom where I slept, Lanes Prince Albert, Beauty of Kent and Bramley at first, then later one called Burnott we got from my grandfather. Pa knew how to propagate by cuttings or layering. Wall Victoria plums were the best I have ever tasted. Later still a pear tree was introduced but that was after my day, also Loganberries.

As we near Lent I am reminded that we did have pancakes. Other items of food were associated with places. Parkins with Masham and perhaps brandy snaps (wafers). Large sweet white biscuits made by Aunty Lydia in Burrill, fish of various kinds, including crab, with Staithes. Raspberries with Sessay as Edith and I had a treat there. Curds with Burrill, as after the cow had calved there were what was called Beastlings (the first lot of milk) and this made good curds for pies, but mother knew how to make that anytime, along with lemon curd for pies.

Easter eggs were dyed; first a candle was used to write on the eggshell, initials etc., then the egg was hard boiled in either coffee or onion water. At Harrogate we got pigs 'trotters' feet as jelly while Mother teased Mr John about his love for tripe when he got it in the market.

The main lot of flowers had an interesting beginning. A trench was dug and was filled with 'night soil' for we had no W.C. When filled in it was the site for the row of sweet peas. One of my jobs was to 'pick those with buds' so that mother could take them to Harrogate on the first train. Sweets were associated with Harrogate as we had no shop for most of the time (one was tried but failed). I think my favourite was toffee at fourpence per quarter pound. Occasionally Pa would make some at home—he liked to add vinegar for some reason and lacking fresh he used some from pickled onions with queer result. I hope that was true, I'm not sure—it may have been his making cough cure.

We had a hand coffee grinder, a sort of box with a handle on top, beans were dropped in and the handle turned for special occasions, but later I recall they had Camp Coffee—a syrup not like the real thing. Mother was very particular about the table when we had visitors and always had cube sugar on the table and milk could be poured from a crockery 'cow'.

Washing day called for an early start, for the fire had to be lit in the washhouse or, as we called it, the copper-house. The set-pot was actually made of copper in some early ones. The fire place under the set pot had a little iron door and that adjusted the draught. All kinds of rubbish could be used, as

46

well as wood or coal. Incidentally we used one in the Starbeck house and with the wind in a certain quarter it 'went mad' and boiled over. So Edith would call me from my study to help.

Sunlight Soap came in long bars and was cut to suit, whites were boiled and lifted out with a 'copper stick' the water having been supplied from large rainwater tubs in the yard. Transferred to a wooden tub the clothes were 'possed' with the use of a 'Peggy stick.' This was formed from a small round stool-like wooden base with a centre post and crossover handle. Some people had a posser without the legs. When washed and rinsed the clothes were taken to a wooden tub before the large iron upright mangle. A formidable object about five feet high with a strong spring controlled by a wheel bearing down on wooden rollers: the handle on the wheel at the end being turned by me when old enough to help.

Whites were improved by the use of a 'dolly blue' or square of blue, and collars etc. were then starched in Robin's Starch. Reckets blue and Coleman's starch comes to mind. There was also Lifeboy soap and there was an advert in the waiting room at the station that amused me. Picture a tramp with a dirty face saying "when a child I used PEAR'S SOAP since then I have used no other." For some drastic cleaning there was Carbolic Soap and later (I think) there was RINSO, a powder. Water was transferred from boiler to tub with a 'lading tin' as we called it—ladle would be correct. There were clothes posts on the side of the line for drying. Inside they were aired on a clotheshorse frame before the open fire. 59 Station Parade had a drying rack hoisted up to the kitchen ceiling by pulley and rope, and I made one for the Starbeck house. Years later we had a gas boiler and metal tub until we got the electric washing machine.

For ironing an old blanket was folded and placed on the table—there were no ironing board. Irons were heated before the open fire and could then be placed in a thin metal sheath. Testing for heat was vital and the iron would be held near the face to test it. That was where starched items showed up. The handle of the iron was covered by a thick 'iron-cloth'. Two or more irons were used to meet the need for re-heating. We wore starched collars to school. I believe delicate fabrics were washed with Soap flakes. Mother wore a 'harden' (hessian) apron for washing day but a white one other days, except Sunday.

One amusing side light on the wash-house was that our neighbour named Wells used theirs as a sort of 'second home. ' I think it was after Spring Cleaning, a big ritual in each home, they spent their evenings in the washhouse, and when I stayed with Mrs Wells on Wednesdays it was there. It had an oven.

Economics

A rather too fancy a term for our financial position and its results. I do not remember money being talked about in our home. If there were difficulties, and there must have been, they were hidden from us. Friday night was Pa's pay-day and mother had the home tidy, flowers on the table and a clean white apron. The pay packet was handed over and Pa had his little share to put away. He did not smoke, so it would be saved for a special need. The house rent would be small and he had,

I think, two free passes on the railway and Privilege Tickets for the family. I believe half a single for the double journey. Later my 'pass' to Thirsk would be cheap. From time to time an engine driver would kick off lumps of coal from the engine as he passed. We picked them up with no thought of dishonesty. We were part of the "Company" as the N. E. R. was called, so what? There was a strange loyalty within the Company in both ways, and men were ever ready to respond in fog or accident to go the second mile to keep trains running on time. I have mentioned elsewhere that Pa would probably have £2 per week and the farm men £1/10/-.

We each had a money box, Norman's being a fancy metal house-like one and mine a red Pillarbox. The only way to get coins out was by use of a knife blade through the slot! There were perks from the railway as old wooden sleepers came cheap and we cut them up for firewood. As soon as I was big enough to hold one end of a crosscut saw the other end was taken by Pa, Mother or Norman and drawn back and forth until the cut was made—hard work. Signal men were better off and worked 8 hour shifts so some got extra work on a farm in season. Pa worked, I think, 7 a.m. to 5 p.m. with a break for breakfast and dinner. Saturday was half day. One year he took evening work and we all shared the task of reducing seedling turnips to one per six inches or so. If Pa was working about the house in an evening Mother always made a point of being at hand to help, if at all possible.

School closed for the potato picking week. Us children joined women from Helperby in the dirty job of picking. In early days a plough split the row and we had to go seeking potatoes and putting them in an old pail. When older as I was big I got the job of 'teeming' full pails on to a cart. Heavy work. I believe we got 7/6d a day. Pickers had to keep up with the fastest picker. I believe at first we shared a row. For a short period I sold papers at Pilmoor station as trains made that possible for a while. We were allowed to go 'gleaning' when the potato harvest was over and rain revealed leftovers; we collected them for home use or for hen food. Pa was a local preacher and cycled many miles, but no contribution was made to him or others. Often a good meal in a farmers house was provided. When old enough I got odd jobs. On one occasion I was sent to Sessay station to collect some sheep. It would be about 4 miles. All went well as I was helped to start the sheep on the homeward way until we came to a T junction and they did not know the way. However I got them rounded up and safely to Pilmoor moor where they scattered and I had to go for the shepherd. I think both he and the porter at the station took a dim view of a lad being sent on such an errand. The farmer at the Grange by that time was a Mr White. I think he had farmed in Canada and was good at cutting corners. He it was that put me on a big 'International' tractor to steer the 'binder' round the field at harvest time. Pity poor Mr Craven on the binder seat behind me!

During school holidays I cycled the 22 miles to Burrill when old enough and often was taken out to help my grandfather. He showed me how to prune etc. and I worked with him quite happily. He would give me sixpence or more on occasion. Once when he was unable to cut the lawn I was sent but handed over payment to Grandad for he needed the money. While there I was taken one day to use a horse rake on the hay field. I had never been in sole charge of a horse before or worked a rake. I was given brief instructions—seated above the rake I had to put my foot on a metal step when the rake was to be lifted. It needed to be timed to give long straight rows of hay. I did not get on too well, I had no watch and went home with the horse when I thought I had done enough. Later I was told the farmer refused to pay me as it was not good enough. My grandfather agreed and gave me some money in lieu. I loved him dearly. Working for the same farmer I was leading full carts of hay to the stack-yard. Coming to a depression the weight of the cart was lifting the horse off his feet. I hung on to his head and he came to earth a bit shaken—all was well. On another occasion the men had failed to load correctly and I had to steer the cart up the side of the road to avoid a spillage. When I got to the stack-yard with the load leaning over the men there cried out 'Oh it's pigged.' Odd phrases abounded.

Our people were always most generous, giving away a good deal of the vegetables they grew. Mother never refused a tramp a bit of food. He was told to sit on the fence outside and she would give him bread and dripping, and a mug of tea.

Looking back I am thankful for all that my parents did for me. Their support all through life was of the highest quality and I thank God upon every remembrance of them. Later in life when I was a Missioner I heard someone say to mother 'you must be proud of him.' She replied, 'We are thankful. He was dedicated at birth. '

Looking back I realise just how hard my mother had to work. We had one large living room with stone floor and the front door opened on to it—no porch. Local land was light so that some days light sand would blow across the field in clouds.

No modern means of clearing the dust, no electricity or gas. I have described washing day and baking day was just as busy as bread was baked for the week. Pies, cakes etc. for Yorkshire teatime all done in a side oven controlled by a damper. My father swept the chimney and I just remember someone going on the roof to let down means of cleaning but then he got a set of rods, but again dust everywhere.

Spring Cleaning and Autumn Cleaning were in fashion and we got lime which was applied to the ceiling year after year until a thick layer had to be scraped off.

There was a fair sized kitchen and a large cool 'pantry' but again no modern means of keeping food fresh. I remember that occasionally a pie would appear with mould on it.

Clip rugs had to be taken out and shaken and I used to hate coming home from school to find the place up-side-down for cleaning. When we were older we could help a little.

I recall that mother had her daily Bible Reading notes but she did not have time to read much. On Sunday afternoon she would pick up a magazine and then fall asleep.

Apart from my fathers spell of illness we kept pretty well but he often had bad head aches and now I know he must have had migraine as did Norman and then his daughter Dorothy.

When the weather was fine, mother loved to get into the garden, for she inherited a love of growing things from her father. She always had plants on both window sills and I recall with pleasure her success. Primula seeds were sown and cared for until full of flowers, for the light was so good. I recall getting a rash on my hands from touching the leaves, so I have avoided them.

Mother was in charge of the hens, as we called what are now termed chickens. Chickens were newly hatched. If we had a cock, then we could use our own eggs for what was called 'sitting'. A broody hen would be given a dozen eggs on which to sit. Young chickens needed care and if there was doubt about the young chick mother would bring it in and put it in flannel by the fire until it picked up.

Money values remained stable through my childhood and youth, not that I knew much about them at the time. I think we reckoned four dollars to the pound. Postage had long been 1d for letters and cards and book post ½d but there was a rise and the card cost 1d and letters 1½d for many years. Mother sent us a card to 5 Kyrle Road 19.7.38 for 1d, they were on holiday at Staithes. I recall the 1926 General Strike. My father was a member of the N. U. R. and was on strike with the rest. We heard the occasional train making its slow way on the main line manned by strike-breakers. I came in for criticism at work over it. It failed in support of the miners. Farm workers had no active Union and got what they could.

There was some charity supported by the gentry. When Mr Greaves, a farmer, died leaving a big family, they were housed in a keepers cottage, and my people did what they could to help.

As a child I had a deep desire to play a musical instrument and my parents gave me a mouth organ, a 'tin whistle' etc., but I had no tutor. About the time I left school I cycled 8 miles to get piano lessons from the minister's wife, but we only had an organ. That effort ended when I left home to work for my uncle.

Chapter 3

Sessay School

I did not go to Sessay School until I was six.

We started in a small classroom at that school—it was fairly modern and there was also the main hall. I wasn't long in the infants and then I moved next door into the main hall. The rest of the hall was for the children from 9 to 14. We sat side-on and had a Miss Rose, who wasn't a fully-trained teacher but was very kind. At that time a Mr Richardson was Head-master and he was pretty strict. Ron Potter and I sat together and we misbehaved. Miss Rose sent us to the Head and he caned us both. We came back and sat on our hands, cried our eyes out, and I remember Miss Rose saying, very kindly really, "Well it was your fault; you shouldn't have done it." I recall that the first cane was black at the end, someone had tried to burn it!

Frank Craven had a stutter and one day he came late to Sessay school. It must have been in my fairly early days in the big room. Of course he had to go before the Headmaster, who, in front of the whole school, asked him why he was late. Poor Frank said, stuttering"P-p-please sir, there's a p-p-plane down in P-p-p-pick's farm"—an aeroplane had landed near the Grange. Mr Richardson asked him to repeat it. He wanted Frank to say "Mr Pick's farm" but Frank didn't cotton onto that. So he started all over again. The rest of the school was in fits and we were enjoying it, poor Frank standing there in sore trouble saying "P-p-p-p". I don't know the outcome but later we saw that plane, a little biplane, and it wasn't far from the farmhouse in the big field. Local men held onto the wings.

The pilot pulled the propeller down and started it, got in and the men let go and off he went. There was an aerodrome on the way from Thornton Bridge to Boroughbridge, just over the hill on the right hand side; there was a small building there for donkey's years and a few acres we called 'the aerodrome'.

Charlie Wood came from Little Sessay and was short tongued, we teased him but I think he enjoyed being the centre of attention. We asked him his name and address—C W Fulham's Farm, Sessay—came out like this "Tarley Bud, Pummem's Parm, Tedder." One day he brought a magnifying glass and used the sun to burn a hole in the lining of his cap. He said "Wilt Bot mell it"—"Will the boss smell it."

Soon the Head retired and we had lady teachers.

We must have looked an odd lot as far as dress is concerned. We were all poor together so did not notice it. Farm men got 30 shillings a week, a tied cottage, free potatoes and skimmed milk. My father probably had £2 a week and the advantage of cheap travel.

I never had 'shop' clothes until quite a big boy. My mother made shorts out of khaki cloth, and I think a jacket. Long stockings, blue 'fisherman's Guernsey', hard collar and an old military cap or balaclava topped all. We were permitted to run out of school to see our first aeroplane.

As a wedding party left the church we greeted them and they threw coppers for which we scrambled. Games came and went, football and cricket—home made bat—in season, but why marbles, whip and top, 'last across' etc. —who set the time? Very occasionally a caravan came and the girls were taught cooking. In Lent a weekly church service, enough to

55

put a child off church going for life! Each day a hymn which we 'picked up' from older children, so often did not understand what we were singing—why did it not have a city wall? I might have mentioned that we sang 'twice one are two' etc. in our first year. Slates and slate pencils were the order of the day for years. It was all a bit of a bore and I was often in trouble.

One less happy memory was of Lent. The older scholars were marched to the nearby church, for our school was C. of E. There we tried to sing a dirge which I still remember began "Forty days and forty nights, Thou wast tempted in the wild." I am sure that service was enough to put a child off for life. We sang "New every morning is the love" at the beginning of the day in school. We were never taught it but 'picked it up' and failed to understand what we were singing. Whatever did "furnish all we ought to ask" mean? (The hymn usually begins "Timely. . .") We had to learn the catechism and the creed, though I felt free church and never quite made the grade. I was not being prepared for the usual confirmation anyway.

As a boy I was tremendously interested in botany. Pilmoor was a real mine for anyone interested in botany. In the pond near the post box there were the insectivorous plants Butterwort and Bladderwort. The big Moor pond was covered in Bogbean. There were also Bee Orchids. A professor from Ripon came out for the day once to look at what there was. Towards the evening he came to our house and asked my mother if she knew where they could get a meal. My mother put on a meal, tea, for them and she told the professor that she had a son—me—who was mad on botany. Afterwards he sent me a a book of wild flowers, which I have treasured ever since.

Strange to say I was bullied. My brother having gone to school with George Welbourne and others at Priory School, York at about eleven, my father put together parts to form a ladies cycle, sit up and beg type, and I suppose the other children were jealous so they made sure I did not pass them on the way home. If I tried I was pulled off by one of the older girls. One day I put my foot out and she ran into it. Not at school next day, I thought I had killed her but she returned, nothing was said but from then on I cycled home unmolested. My last year was a waste of time and I was pleased to leave the day before my 14th birthday.

In contrast my brother had a good education, got a good job in York and enjoyed close friendship with Frank Hick who began Railway life at Boroughbridge and wrote 'That was my Railway.' I tried to get into Priory at about eleven but being shy was end of queue and told the class was full.

A mixed school, we learned to read and write but the level of education cannot have been very high, though I managed fractions and decimals quite well. Perhaps I underrate the teaching. One joy was the help I had with the identification of plants. The head, a Mrs Smith, never tired of finding the answer, as I took rare flowers to her. Toward the end of my school life I was left to do as I liked. I was tall for my age being better fed than many and it would seem the head teacher saw little point in spending time with older scholars. Farmer's children either went off to better schools or just left to take their place on the farm confident of a good future. Others left to work for a few shillings either in a 'Place,' domestic service for girls, or on the farm being 'hired' for a year at a time.

Chapter 4

At a Loose End

Leaving school the day before I was 14, I had no work. I did not want to work on a farm as I was afraid of horses and had seen something of the hard life a boy could have there. One memory is of a boy from the South whose language we found hard to understand. He was like a lonely slave and we had a succession of these locally. I fear we did not help them as they were strangers.

During this period I would wander the moorland round my home always ready to get a rabbit, or better still to pick up a pheasant that had hit the telegraph wire. I did not think it wrong to take eggs and my mother did not find them unwelcome. I knew the moor like the back of my hand, could roam freely on the line side or on the Old Line without let or hindrance. The 'Back Moor' as we called the area round the Delta pond, west of the railway and over to Pilmoor Hall land, was a game area at that time; carefully fenced in, and frequently patrolled by the gamekeepers and occasionally by the Helperby Bobby. Unknown to my parents I trespassed, looking for the unwary rabbit in its sett, or a nest of Teal-duck eggs. Had I been caught, at best it would have been a family interview with Mr Topham, or at worst, being taken by the assistant or police as having a catapult on enclosed land etc. The nearest thing to poaching I ever dared do, knowing I would not have my parents support. The most foolish thing I did was to set a wagon moving on the Moor siding, as we had done as a 'gang' of boys some time before. I could not stop it and had a vision of the trouble I would be in if it went through the Moor side gate.

However I did manage to brake, made sure it was safe and never was tempted again. The other 'folly' was not of my making. Hearing a tractor at work on the Grange land I went to watch the harvest in progress. Mr White was driving an International tractor with Mr Craven on the Massey Harris Binder. He called me to him, showed me how to steer and left us to it. It might have had disastrous results, for the big drive wheel on the binder got blocked with weed and Mr Craven had to come and reverse the whole contraption and run back to take control of the Binder. I loved it but he must have had a very bad time. It was as well it was not a big field.

I still remember being in Bedale market at the time for hiring workers. I was a big lad but only 13 when a stranger asked my Grandfather if I was for hire. I can still feel the mixture of fear and relief that I was not yet 14. Imagine what it must have been like to be handed over at 14 to leave home and join a hardworking family at the beck and call of everyone. Hired for a year there was no release. Not quite a slave but very nearly.

I did not want to work on a farm because I was afraid of horses. One had taken a nip at my brother, and I had seen what a bad tempered one could do with his hind legs. So I was afraid of both ends! When I had briefly worked with them on school holidays at Burrill I had not been much good. One day set to work a horse-rake, I made such a mess of it that the farmer refused to pay me!

My parents had helped my mother's brother George to set up in business with a horse and flat cart. Now he had two shops in Bedale and a big house named Victory House (and Store) a car and a van for deliveries. My uncle made a monthly visit by Ford car to deliver a sack of white flour and other groceries. On 3rd March 1925 he said "Everybody's down with 'flu and we're in a terrible mess, can Stanley come and help?" My mother packed my bag and I went just like that the same day. So at 14 I left Pilmoor for Bedale to become errand boy, van boy and general dogsbody. Sometimes I was even allowed to drive the van along farm tracks and the like. A wonderful treat for a boy of 14 in those days. The work was hard, and on Saturdays we worked from 8.0 am to 8.0 pm. I had my keep and five shillings pocket money.

My mother had packed my bag when I left home. Mother kissed me when I left, which for Yorkshire people in those days was quite memorable. When I opened that bag I found she had included my Bible which I had never really read, and my Methodist hymnbook. It was there, in the loneliness of my little bedroom that, coming face to face with myself and seeing that I was already an active sinner, I knelt to ask God's forgiveness. I knew the WAY and began in rather a shaky fashion to walk in it.

Was it the sight of that Bible or home sickness that drove me to my knees, I don't know; but from then on what had been a formal agreement with my parent's religion became a living relationship with my Saviour and slowly I began to change. It was a very different person that returned to Pilmoor from the one that left to work in Bedale. I have been changing ever since—or growing.

Looking back, I now see this job as a pattern of my life. Like all errand boys I was known to dawdle and even on occasion to fail to deliver the goods, a reflection of my many adult failures. However it has been a great privilege to be any kind of messenger for such a gracious divine master for more than 65 years.

In their way they were quite kind to me but I was more on a level with the two servant girls "living in" than with the family. There was a fair sized grocery shop and across the Market Place a corner shop selling sweets. Apart from turning the ice cream maker in season I had nothing to do with the sweet shop apart from a little bag of unsellable sweets each week!

I think we worked from 8.0 a.m. to 6.0 p.m. except Saturday when it was open until 8.0 p.m. and often I had to deliver groceries by hand barrow after that. It was heavy work and I once carried in a bag of maize of 2 cwts and my older workmate had to put it on the scales to convince me.

One of the good things was there were motors—a one ton van we used to deliver groceries to remote farms and another Ford tourer the family owned. My Uncle was a local preacher. On occasion I had to go with him in that car as he went to get orders. It was then I learned to smoke—not much but when we were given cigs. , as we called them.

I attended the Methodist Bible Class and on one occasion was asked to prepare a 'Paper' at the Guild. It was on the armour of the Christian and I was told there was none for the back! A young minister took an interest in me and had me read the lesson. On one such occasion I had difficulty with 'sufficeth us'! I suppose I was fairly happy but as time went on was often called to work on odd jobs after hours etc. while the boys of the family got off free. By the way, I was taken to the Railway Centenary occasion at Darlington in 1925.

There came a sad day when I heard my Uncle speak of one of the maids in a wrong way and I went and told her. That ended my life there in a most unhappy fashion. I was sent to Burrill to my grandfather's for a week and worked at the shop each day in tearful fashion until I was put on the train for home—Jan. 23rd 1926. It was a very tearful time and I was in utter disgrace but eventually all was forgiven and later on I was able to ask my uncle to come and preach at my first Mission Hall.

So once again I was out of work. My brother took a dim view of my condition! By this time he was working in an office in York. My mother was most kind—we were always very close. I don't remember my father being cross with me at that time though he had a very short temper in those days.

Chapter 5

Castlegate Garage

I was now back home and without a job. But not for long. One of the friends of the Methodist Chapel to which we went on Sunday afternoons was a lovely Christian lady. Although she never said so, I believe it was she who arranged for me to get work as a sort of apprentice at her son's garage—Mr Robert Eden at Castlegate Garage in Thirsk. I was paid 7/6 a week and it involved a train journey (cheap) and a mile walk from station to town or a more frequent eight mile cycle ride. I had half a day off on Wednesday and worked Saturday 'keeping shop' so missed cricket except in an evening. I loved the work, dirty though it was.

I think I worked from 8.30 a.m. to 5.30 p.m. with Wednesday half day. Monday was market day and so that was our busy day and I was very happy to be learning a trade. There was one elder lad, Norman Saddler and we got on well. I started 15th March 1926 so had been out of work for two months. I did a bit of farm work and for some days drove a tractor at harvest time.

I had a 'pass' to go to work on the morning train from Pilmoor Station to Thirsk but that station is a mile from town. There was a bus—I seem to remember going with my mother when it was horse-drawn, but by then it would be a motor – but it cost fourpence so I walked or ran. Most days I cycled and sometimes I would eat my sandwiches at the home of my Great Uncle John and his wife. I was very happy working at the garage.

My boss heard that the Police Inspector got a driving licence for his son at 16 and applied for one for me. I had to go to Northallerton and drive before the Chief Constable, just round the big car park. He said I had not done enough, but my boss said "well, he has driven here today." Instead of a 'charge' I got my licence, limited to 'North Riding only'. That licence is now in the Motor Museum at Beaulieu.

When I was part of the threefold 'team' of drivers, I was sent one day to collect two ladies from Thirsk and they asked me to take them to Sowerby (fee 2/-). I was given a visiting card and told to take it to the door of a big house. The maid took it on a silver tray and sent me away. They had done a Victorian 'Visit to new people', I suppose, for they then asked to be driven home and gave me a tip of sixpence. Was that the last time a 'visiting card' was delivered?

Before long I was going with my father to read the lessons when he was engaged to preach on the Wesleyan and Primitive Methodist local circuits. Methodism encouraged lay preachers, and by the time I was 18 I had begun to preach in various village chapels. The 'plan' said I was on trial, but I think it was the congregation that was being tried. It was during this period that I met a local minister who was also a Scout Master and he introduced me to Scouting, an interest which was to last many years.

About this time my brother bought a motor cycle – the Raleigh was delivered and I was taught to drive it (if that is the term) and then introduced it to Norman!

One of the few notes in my diary was 'Ess. of ginger 3 drams, Ess. of cayenne 1 dram, Ess. of lemon ½ dram, Burnt sugar 2oz.'

so I must have been sent to the chemist for our ginger wine mixture!

We sold petrol; aviation petrol in gold tins and also benzole mixture, which came in iron barrels and I had the job of measuring off into tins. My first note of price is one shilling and sixpence half penny per Gallon and that would be for Russian Oil Product (R.O.P.). Eventually we had a pump installed.

1927

My only note was 'left Bedale 2 years 3.3.27' (an event to remember!) until 14.3 'one year at garage'—a happier note. The next was that petrol had come down Benzol mx.1/6 petrol 1/5½ it had been up to 1/8!

About this time I note I had a Douglas motor cycle—no details: but I think it cost £5.0.0. It was W.D. (war dept.) so may have seen service in France! It leaked oil and seems to have brought problems but I was learning! I did a major overhaul of the Raleigh for Norman. There is much detail of car washing, big ends, axle renewal, stub axle renewal, new wings fitted and the occasional tip.

On wet days I went by train but got wet coming home some days, but kept fit.

We had French cars, a large 'Closed' car a bit like a big London Taxi, an 'Open' Darraque and another very fine Talbot-Darraque. The family where Mr Eden lived-in as a paying guest had an open two seater Star car with two seats which could be opened like a boot, known then as a Dickey-seat! This was the most modern of the stock. By 30th March I proudly recorded that I had driven the 'Closed car' on a station run. Imagine me in peak cap etc.

On April 2nd I got a rise to eight shillings and sixpence and Mr Eden paid 1/6d National Insurance. It seems that in May I went rook shooting and often record that I took Mr Eden to his brother's farm for him to go shooting.

June 5th began a very mixed period which I will not go into with much detail. Harrogate Town Mission went as a party to my home and a very attractive girl and her mother were with the party. The father had been killed in the war and my parents were always offering holidays to such needy folk.

I suppose I had led a rather lonely life, though my family were most kind and supportive. I have an early recollection of hugging the family cat, which had lost a leg on the railway but still managed to catch small rabbits, and telling her my childish troubles. I recall too finding her giving birth to kittens. My boyhood friend Clare, the son of the gamekeeper employed by the Coates family of Helperby Hall, had left for work at Guisborough, so I had few real friends.

I went to a mixed school, but after school days I had little contact with the opposite sex apart from the two maids at Bedale, so the advent of Marion Ratner overwhelmed me. Letters went back and forth and we met whenever possible.

At this time Norman took me to Staithes for a holiday. I went on the back of his motorcycle. We saw a coble being towed in which might have been blown out to sea, visited Runswick Bay, etc. On the Saturday I got a telegram from Mr Eden to get back to work Monday 9.30. We left early and ran into icy roads. I was thrown along the road and ran back to lift the cycle from Norman, but we were not seriously hurt.

It seems I kept up my interest in wild flowers. Years before I had helped Edith to get (I think) 70 for a badge. I note I had found four bee Orchids on the moor. Harrogate Town Mission folk were at Pilmoor, August 1st, and later Marion and her mother were there on holiday. I was very much in love but as time went by it became clear that Marion had other friends. After all she was not 15 until October. By the end of the year the friendship was at an end. It is worthy of note that I read the lesson at Sessay Chapel 7th August 1927 and that a new minister came who was to play a big part in our lives. Rev Peter T. Hutchison was from Shetland and he introduced me to Scouting. Later he was to take our wedding. By October I record that I gave the address at Sessay, and on the 11th Mother and Dad had their silver Wedding celebration.

Scouting

Rev Peter T Hutchison set up a troop which met in two places at least and occasionally in a third, the third one being the reading room at Pilmoor. We met to begin with in the schoolroom at Helperby chapel. I think every boy of scouting age from Pilmoor joined the troop. I don't think they ever had cubs, but we had good fun and I learnt quite a lot, though it came along in my middle teens and I was much too old to be a scout so I was a lone Rover and eventually PTH's assistant. The outstanding thing was that he arranged for us to go to the world Jamboree at Arrow Park, Birkenhead and so Pilmoor boys were part of the representation of the British nation among many and we had a wonderful time; of course sleeping in tents, we had our own gear and it was a very damp, muddy arrangement. We couldn't help the weather but we had one wonderful day when we got up quite early and got settled at a vantage point to see the chief, Baden Powel, however you like to pronounce it, and the Prince of Wales who never did actually become king. I so well remember squatting there over quite a period of time when some Scottish lads and their scouter came and sat in front of us. PTH, who as a Shetlander was not very fond of Scottish people, blew his top and there was a first class set to. Result: departure of the Scottish boys and their leader and not a very friendly atmosphere I'm afraid. But after all's said and done we had got there in very good time. The joke that went around was that a boy scout hat, those flat things that only scouts would be seen dead in, was found sitting on the mud and when they lifted it out, there was a small scout under it blowing bubbles. Certainly we did have quite a lot of rain but I've got some quite nice snapshots of those happy days. We had a great time and visited Liverpool, Kirby etc. I note that we must have had a special train to take us from Leeds for two engines are listed and they had a job to pull a full train.

The time came when Helperby boys lost interest and so we carried on at Pilmoor. After PTH departed to be minister of another church then I carried it on as First Pilmoor, but of course before very long I felt called to go into training as an evangelist. I was encouraged by PTH to do this and I think I may well have been supported as I went to Cliff College having no money and no other known support, unless my parents managed to scimp some little extra. I shall never know.

My driving took me further afield now, and I took a party to Whitby in their bullnosed Morris Cowley. Two ladies from a local shop kept their car in the Central Garage and I looked after it and kept it clean.

On Oct. 24th I bought my second Douglas motorcycle. It cost me £8.10.0 and was still a belt drive but it took Edith and me to Staithes. At the time I think we were just life long friends and no more! I note that Sydney brought Edith to Pilmoor on the back of his new B.S.A. 250 cc. It is clear at this time that I was very upset, but I wrote in my diary "Seek ye first the Kingdom etc." so I was growing up! Marion's mother was most kind and pointed out that as she put it I was experiencing calf love! I don't remember coming across this phrase later in life, but she was right.

At the end of the year I went by train to Bedale to get to Burrill and noted that I wanted to join in the prayer time but was too shy. On Dec. 18 I noted that I had overcome this at Sessay.

1928 began with my giving the address at Sessay and preaching at Dalton on Josh 1 v 9 — I needed courage too. Jan 21st saw me on one of our frequent visits to 29 Station Parade. Evidently I avoided the Mission but saw Marion later at 29.

Feb. 1st I made a note to "Trust in the Lord and wait patiently for Him." Noted Matt 7 v 34, "Take no thought etc." and Matt. 7 v 11, a verse that was to mean a great deal to me later in life. The gift of the Holy Spirit. Evidently I was reading my Bible.

Feb. 12th I went with Dad to Helperby and took communion for the first time.

Being very much a 'railway child' I recorded seeing an accident happen at the station. A goods train had been reversed into a siding to make way for the main line train. If there was room for 100 wagons then there were 101 in the train. The engine pushed and pushed to clear the 'trap', the signal-man then opened the trap. The compressed wagons then pushed the front wheels of the engine off the trap. I watched later operations during the night!

An interesting item re. money! I was given a Christmas box at work and noted "was half for the other lad." Some days later I note I gave him half, namely 2/6 and the same day I was given 2/- — another lesson for the future. At this time I spoke at Sessay on Heb. 6 v 18 "The Hope set before us and the anchor of the soul."

On March 26th I noted that it was Edith's 18th birthday. Good Friday seems to have been 'one of those days'. I went to Harrogate and took Edith to Burrill. Mr Turner took Mrs Turner to Pilmoor, then took Dad to Burrill in the sidecar. On the way home they had a smash and both were thrown out.

April saw me at Topcliffe with the minister P.T.H. and reading the lesson etc. and on the 29th. I took Edith to Burrill, then to her home and the Town Mission. I spoke in the Open Air Meeting at the Opera House corner for the first time.

I appear to have constructed a radio (wireless!) and started going to the scout meetings in Helperby.

In May I took Marion to Burrill and a long ride via Masham etc. On June 2nd I left Thirsk at 4.0 and got to Staithes at 6.0, 42 miles, which gives some idea of our speed at that time. Crossing the village at 12 midnight we were stopped by police. Leaving at 8.30 on Sunday, home at 11.0 a.m.

One Sunday I took Pa to preach and record that we got home in time to hear the service from St. Martin's in the Field on wireless – quite an event.

Norman was paying frequent visits to Staithes and Sarah-Lizzie was at Pilmoor from time to time.

June 17th. I spoke on "Rejoice evermore, pray and give thanks", at Marten le Moor.

From then on the diary is a blank after one last visit to Marion. My Grandfather was 71 on Aug. 22nd 1928. I sent Marion a scarf for her birthday Oct. 5th. Holiday with Edith & family at Staithes August.

October 13th one of the high spots began. Stayed the night with the Scott family. Next morning we left at 6.30 for London. Annie Scott drove to Doncaster, and I drove from there. We had one puncture. This adventure began with one of my frequent jokes. Learning that Mr & Miss Scott and her boy friend were going to the Motor Show I said 'Do you want a driver?' They had not intended to drive. We stayed at the National Hotel at 7/6d per night bed and breakfast.

Monday by tube to Motor Show. Prices are priceless! Tea 1/9d at ABC, tube 5d, Show entry 5/-, catalogue 1/-, Lunch 1/-, Tea 9d, to Oxford St. Tower etc. Parliament Sq. etc. Tuesday. Wednesday to the Zoo in the morning to Embankment, Westminster etc. afternoon. Lunch cost 2/- ! Zoo entry 1/- .

On the Thursday we left Russell Square at 9.30 and we got to Thirsk at 6.50. Mr Eden had given me a £5 note the first I had seen. He said it was "to hold your end up!" This was quite an adventure at that time and of course I was only a little over 18 at the time.

I note that Edith's boy friend Harry Fuller died on Nov. 24th. He was said to have sinusitis. So simple to cure today.

Christmas 1928 the Turner family were at Pilmoor as usual and also Mrs Fuller and daughter Gwen. How like my dear parents to invite the very sad sister and mother for the holiday period. Females in the front bedroom, males in the back bedroom. But what a wonderful cook/housekeeper my mother must have been. The diary was little used but ends with the quote "To thine own self be true, etc."

1929 began with the Scout investiture and the arrival of my Assistant Scoutmaster's warrant. Saturday 19th I had a half day off for the first time and went to Harrogate and to Starbeck at night to the Mission.

Visits to Harrogate became more frequent but Sundays were largely given over to preaching. I note that I began to preach in Thirsk and Boroughbridge Circuits, as well as for the small Thirsk Primitive Methodist Circuit, of which Sessay was one church. Preaching for Wesleyans made going to Cliff easier as the Methodist Union came later.

It is interesting to note some of the village names in which I preached. Bagby, Borrowby, Sandhutton, Marton le Moor, Carlton Miniot, Minskip and the larger church at Topcliffe. Occasionally I note 8 miles for 6 people! Preaching increased during the year; on a few occasions I took three services. Once I went to a big church in Pateley Bridge to stand in for a minister; how they got my name I don't know.

On 26th March I note that I had sent handkerchiefs to Edith. At that time we were just good friends, almost like brother and sister - no more.

Preaching at Staveley I note that Sydney (Edith's brother) and his girl friend joined me and sang a duet. Sydney, his father, my father and I all appeared on Methodist Plans, as they were called. The moon phases were shown as special events needed some light! People were a bit confused—H. Turner, J.H. Turner, S. Turner and S.M. Turner, some on 'full plan,' others visitors, and me 'on trial'!

Scouts were taking a good deal of time but numbers were small. There was a camp during the summer.

In April I had an accident that might have had far reaching consequences. Riding my belt drive Douglas out of the garage I met the young lady Miss Scott on the blind corner. Her driving of the Star car proved good, for I was knocked off my cycle and she stopped her car inches from my leg. Apart from a dented petrol tank there was little damage.

One Sunday in April I went to Harrogate to collect Edith, returned to Minskip to preach and she probably sang and then I took her home and returned to Pilmoor. We were good friends.

In May I went to Harrogate and then with Edith and Gwen Fuller to Starbeck. Edith was friendly with members of the Starbeck Mission Bible Class run by Mr Hawkes. Harry had been a member and one member was still attending when I went as Missionary. Edith was at Pilmoor for Whit, and I took her home.

At this time I wrote to Edith about a holiday. I cannot place this but remember taking her to Staithes on the belt drive Douglas. We went to the usual places, Runswick Bay, Loftus where she had relations, and to Robin Hoods Bay, where we had to leave the cycle at the top of the hill and walk down.

We never seemed to think it might lead to the loss of the cycle. Incidentally I recall the belt broke and out came the tool kit we always carried. A screw punch to hole the belt, spare link to join it up again, and off we went. We were young and care-free and such adventures caused us no concern. I just wonder how we did get by though. I think my parents were on holiday with us. Of course we needed supervision.

Mrs Turner was over from Starbeck and I went for Edith on the 24th. Rev. P. T. Hutchison left for Somerset during the month. I carried on with a Pilmoor Troop but it was not to last long.

October saw me in Harrogate and at Minskip, so once again Edith would share with me in ministry. I was back on the Wednesday after. My father took a dim view of oft repeated visits as I fear we did not dig the garden as much as we might.

I paid another visit to Staithes in November and then noted that Edith and I went to a friend's house for the evening. By the way, Norman took me to Staithes on his B.S.A., we left early, ran into icy conditions, came off, but again were no worse. Dec. 24th saw the Turner family at Pilmoor as usual. On Christmas Day we went to see Mr & Mrs Ireland who used to live at The Grange, Pilmoor, and had my early Sunday school days in their kitchen.

They lived near Crayke and it involved hill climbing. Edith and I were late returning on the Douglas and got our legs pulled but we were still 'just friends.'

I began to love my Bible and was very sure of my faith. I was just 19 when something happened that was to decide my life work. I was attending the Harrogate Town Mission. In the "Watch Night" service in the lower Hall I felt led to surrender my life to Christ. It was as if I had handed him a parcel and He had accepted it. It was as definite as that. As St Paul puts it I became a 'slave of Jesus Christ'. Long after I learned that Edith had made a similar commitment. It was to lead to Cliff and full time Christian service. When my boss at the garage learned I was leaving he said "There will be a business for someone one day". I'm glad I did not stay on!

1930

On the 7th of January I got a letter from Edith asking me to go. I got a half day on the Thursday 9th. and so began a new relationship. I got home at 11.30 that night.

So far I had made all the running and I can understand why Edith was not particularly interested. There was none of the romance of getting to know a new friend. She had known me all her life and knew me "warts and all". It was years later that she told me that her mother, who knew of her reluctance to respond to my attentions, said to her "You are a silly girl, Stanley will make you a good husband." I am thankful to my kind little mother-in-law for her support then and always.

Jan. 12th saw me in Harrogate and Edith going with me to Skelton. We were back at Starbeck in the afternoon.

Letters now began to pass to and from Edith.

Feb. 9th is interesting for I record that I gave three addresses, Bagby, then to Harrogate to share with Sidney services at Killinghall. I note it was 'a good day and one to be very thankful for.'

On the 11th. I wrote to Edith, to say I would be late as I had to work. On the Wednesday I got to Harrogate at 6.25

and we went to Starbeck Mission. 'A good meeting.' Would that be their Anniversary? I don't think I gave an address.

On the 27th. of Feb. I went to York to get the night train to see P.T.H. in Somerset. I got my eyes opened to evil men as sailors were in the compartment. I escaped to another and they got drunk. It was a mail train and very slow. The next morning I had a new railway experience. I had to be in the last coach, which proved to be what is known as a 'slip coach.' As we got to the station our coach was slipped and the main train went on. One man controlled our coach and brought it to rest at the platform.

I was with the family over the weekend and gave an address. I was taken to Beer on the coast etc. by P.T.H. on his motorcycle, then home Tuesday evening. The Turner family were at Pilmoor for the Sunday School prize giving. Sunday School was in Gate House at that time, as it had been for some years.

I think I gave an address at Harrogate Town Mission one Sunday afternoon. Mr Govier was the Missioner and was kind to me. He would have liked me to go to B.T.I. Glasgow where he had been.

In April there is a note about someone making a confession of faith. Edith was with me again to sing at Minskip. It was now quite usual for me to go to Harrogate on my half day and if possible at the weekend. For Easter weekend Edith was brought to Pilmoor and on the Good Friday Sydney, Edith and I went to Burrill. On Easter Day I had to take the Sessay service and Edith went with me to sacrament in the evening.

I now appear to have the third Douglas, an EW bought cheap after a young rider had been killed on it. A much improved model. I note that the 17 miles took 26 minutes.

In May I note that I had sent a letter to Cliff.

It would seem that by this time I was getting requests for dates. Burrill and Bedale are mentioned.

June 24th wrote to Mr Chadwick at Cliff.

In July I attended Burrill Love Feast. These were a feature of earlier Methodism. A special gathering of local Christians from a wide area met together and a glass of water and a special 'love feast biscuit' was passed round. Testimonies were given and a special address. I had always found them emotional occasions as my parents would take part. On July 19th I went for Edith as Mother would have been alone. By this time I think Norman had a small car and took Edith home.

August 3rd Edith and I went to see Grandad and Aunty Lydia at Burrill, and the following day left for Staithes where her parents were on holiday. I took Sarah to work and Edith and I went to Loftus and Redcar. We walked to Runswick Bay by the cliff top. Mother and Dad joined us on the Saturday and I returned on the Sunday and I note it was the best holiday ever.

Chapter 6

Cliff College

I applied to Cliff College the following year and was accepted as a Student.

When I told Mr Eden of my plans he said, "There will be a business here for someone and Norman (the other lad) does not seem interested." In some circumstances this might have been a temptation, but though I loved the work among the cars, and had been happy to work for such a good man, I was not even tempted to alter my course.

It is worthy of comment that I had never been of much use to my parents, financially. They never put anything in my way but gave me every encouragement to go to Cliff. Among the list of books etc. that Cliff required was a Chambers Dictionary. I well remember my future mother-in-law taking me to a second hand bookshop and paying for the copy. I have it still and think of her kindness.

Sept. 17th: To Harrogate for Edith, then to see Grandad and Aunty, back to Harrogate and home—90 miles.

Sept. 29th: Finished at the Garage. Said goodbye to Edith on the 2nd Oct. and left for Cliff. Mother saw me off and I saw Mr & Mrs T. at Harrogate and Norman at Leeds. Met Cliff men at Sheffield. What a welcome we had. Rev. Chadwick, the Principal at the first meeting, then a wonderful prayer meeting. Sunday, Principal at chapel—I seeking to find the fullness the others had yet had to wait.

At Cliff I took the next big step in my spiritual growth. I found about 70 young men dedicated to God and rejoicing in a way that I did not know. I knew a good deal about the Holy

Spirit and was conscious of His gracious work in my life, for it was all of grace that I had got so far. However, I came to know the 'fullness' of the Holy Spirit in an ecstatic experience that was to lead to a quickened mind for study and a more effective ministry. The early excitement passed but the experience stayed and if I have been of any use to God during my life, I date it back to that time.

Nothing on earth could make up for a very limited elementary education in a country school with only two class rooms. But under the guidance of a very remarkable Principal, Samuel Chadwick, who had himself been a 'half-timer' in a mill at the age of 8 but was now a renowned expositor of the Bible comparable with Dr Campbell Morgan, I learned how to study and trust God. Samuel Chadwick was failing in health but we held him in high esteem.

The college course was an intensive one and we worked hard. Our beloved principal said he wished to make us 'students of original research' and to that end he applied what he called 'Monastic discipline'; there was no time for games but we had plenty of exercise for some time was spent working on the estate. Rising bell went at 6.30 a.m. Call at 7.0.

October 9th there is the note PRAISE GOD FOR FULL SALVATION. I now knew the full indwelling of the Spirit.

Cliff supplied preachers for chapels over a wide area. Students without cycles walked up to ten miles to take services; cyclists went up to sixteen miles; just once I went further and was given weekend hospitality by an elderly widow. She treated me as a V. I. P. (very important preacher) and put me in the front room. She soon found that I was much happier in the kitchen helping to wash-up and we had a good weekend.

My first preaching appointment was 16 miles away at Brassington, the second only 12! (Cycle)

I had an interview with Mr Lambert, my tutor, and came away with a new assurance.

There was a visit to Sheffield with the whole college and a great occasion. November 8th, a 20 mile ride to take services and return on the Monday. Exam marks began to get better, 69/100, but some were still low. The rather bold motto at the end of the year was 'live dangerously' but it is qualified as 'Bold aggressiveness for Christ!'

Four days a week we spent half a day on what was called 'manual' and as I was a country lad I was placed in charge of a team to deal with trees. We pollarded and cut up fallen trees for firewood. I quite enjoyed the respite from study and had happy fellowship with Brother Huck. We have written to each other each Christmas since.

1931

Jan 2nd. I left Harrogate at 12.30 for Mill Bridge to Brother Malta's home for a series of special Missions under the leadership of Brother Devonshire—we were all Cliff men.

On the first Saturday I spoke on 'What think ye of Christ' and there was one response at the close. We had prayer meetings each morning, toured the district and visited to get people to attend. I was interested to find I was in the Batley district—my father's home town. On the Sunday two of us took the Sunday School and it seems we took the title 'Sunshine Twins.' We were all rejoicing in the Lord. Brother Snow lived in the district, and it is interesting that he went to China as a Missionary later in life. Each day we went to mills etc. to make known the meetings and to preach, and day by day recorded conversions. The brother of our host and his girl friend were in the meeting one evening and, as we had prayed for them, I looked up as the appeal was made and saw them get up out of their seats. For a moment I thought they were leaving but no! they came forward for counselling.

Jan. 9th. I left for Cliff with Brother Snow and Brother Tulli my Italian friend. I was put in the Extra English class to learn some grammar, as leaving school the day before I was 14, I seem to have missed it! I appear to have looked for a letter from Edith each day and certainly they were usually there!

Feb. 20th, I note that my brother Norman sent me 5/- and think this was to pay for my driving licence, as I had been helping to drive staff cars on occasion and it had run out. One very special day was when I was asked to drive the Principal to and from Willersley Castle.

The end of March brought exams and I note that I had improved over the last term to a marked degree—73, 70, 71, 77. Before Easter, Staff and students conducted an evangelistic campaign in Derby. In addition to big central meetings we were allocated to churches in pairs. My dear Italian friend Renato and I worked in a chapel in the outskirts, taking services, visiting the district and spending some time in the local pub talking to men.

There was one late night central meeting. We met men out of the pubs at closing time and gathered a big crowd in a church. There was much singing, testimonies were given, the gospel was presented in simple terms and about midnight an appeal was made for men to seek salvation. Many made a rather unsteady move to kneel at the communion rail. The rest of the time was spent in counsel and prayer and Renato and I walked back to our 'home' at 2.0 a.m. I recall kneeling on the cobbles after a big open-air meeting to pray with seekers. We were not only being trained in evangelism, we were becoming evangelists.

April 14th I was home, having called for Edith in Harrogate. On the 12th I was invited to be on the platform at the Town Mission and spoke in the Open Air Meeting afterwards. I visited Burrill and returned to Cliff on the 17th. There had been a doubt about my return, but when I saw the Principal he agreed to my return, some difficulty about money (of which I had none) having been overcome. On the 27th I record that Edith had entered upon deeper spiritual blessing. Letters were frequent.

I note that I had to take part in what we called the Clinic. One student preached and half a dozen 'criticised' various aspects. Often the critic got a much harder time from Mr Chadwick than the preacher.

Whit weekend saw the celebrated Anniversary gathering. Thousands came for the Monday and Mum and Dad, Sydney and Edith among them.

I note that on a day off some of us went to the Blue John Mine. It was a remarkable underground experience and I found a little of the Blue Stone.

One sad thing was the death of Mrs Dunning, wife of a tutor.

Mid June saw my marks reaching an average of 68.6 and in his testimonial the Principal said my marks never fell below honours level in my second and third terms, such was the grace of God and their teaching methods.

On June 23rd I left Cliff and note "Praise God for Cliff." On the 24th I had my 21st Birthday party and left for Trek on the 29th. Trek calls for a chapter on its own and ended with us preaching in Leeds and then walking through the night to Cliff at 6.45 a.m., which I listed as being 49 miles, by far our longest trek.

Chapter 7

The Trek

At the end of our training period we were encouraged to take part in an evangelistic "trek". Each team had their blankets, cooking gear etc. loaded on a light covered hand cart. Going out in "faith", the basic trek fund was £1 and the Principal said he would like it back at the end of the three months. We agreed not to take collections, and not to ask for anything other than clean water and shelter for the nights.

Our trek left for a week in Ireland and then to walk across Scotland, preaching most evenings. Irish Methodists made us most welcome and gave us good meals but little money. After Belfast and other large centres walking 80 miles we arrived at Larne to cross to Scotland, when the leader found on going to the port office to book our cart, that the charge was more than was in the Trek Fund. After nearly a year without paid employment as individuals we had little personal cash. However we emptied our pockets and found the required sum. Arriving at the port next morning we were told our 'cart' was a wheelbarrow, so we got our money back.

After trekking 17 miles, a minister let us sleep on his garage floor (we did not sleep in beds, even if it was offered). Next morning he gave us breakfast! After another 13 miles we found a welcome in Girvan. That evening we gathered a crowd of about a hundred after the entertainments closed. Not only did we get a good hearing but all kinds of gifts came to us, including a box of kippers which we boiled in the dixie in which we brewed tea! And so we proved God and the kindness of Scots.

Our method was to seek a crowd. At that time people were familiar with political meetings being held in the open-air. Most towns had a forum. However if we found men outside a factory at lunch time we held a meeting. We did not carry the proverbial 'soap box'. If need be we borrowed a beer box from a pub. With a leader on the box the rest formed the front row. If, as often happened, we had a heckler, that was a real help.

On the side of the trek cart were the words,"We preach Christ and Him crucified" and on the back "1,000 miles of witness," and the location of our next stop. That might be as far away as 25 miles, but often much shorter. Weekends found us in large towns or cities such as Glasgow, Dundee, Edinburgh, Newcastle, or Leeds. People may well have doubted our sanity but could not doubt our sincerity.

It is difficult to know how effective our witness was. I noted that about 180 individuals had responded to our appeal, for long before Billy Graham was asking people to "get up out of their seats" we were asking people to come forward and shake hands with the leader as an indication of their seeking the Saviour. One member of the trek went to theological college and on trek for the three following summers and rejoiced to meet converts going on well. In Harrogate a young man named Ivor came forward to shake my hand. Years later I visited my brother and went to the church where he was Treasurer. There I met the Revd. Ivor now a Methodist Minister. On the last weekend we were in Leeds, on the Monday we trekked all day, held an open-air meeting in the evening, and then set off for Cliff. Walking all night we did 49 miles in total—just to complete a joyous experience, covering about three months.

Trek Diary—1931

This is a transcription of the notebook carried on Trek in 1931. It was not written for publication, and has only been lightly edited.

— ·— ·— ·— ·— ·— ·— ·— ·— ·— ·— ·— ·— ·— ·—

June 29 Monday

Arrived at Southport for dinner via Harrogate & Preston. Meeting at 3.0. Good crowd but not too struck on the speakers. Open air meeting on South Shore at 5.30. A number of testimonies and three hands up in answer to Mr Lambert's appeal—stayed on after to see them—two ladies were RC—rather difficult—young lady from against Bolton—Annie & Eunice Braithwaite from Edgeworth. Second girl came out in answer to Bro H appeal. Great time & crowd unwilling to leave.

Meeting inside—came in late—got a real message on sacrificial service—real giving a hand for another.

Supped & fun with DWL, JIB & NGD & so to bed with one blanket.

— ·— ·— ·— ·— ·— ·— ·— ·— ·— ·— ·— ·— ·— ·—

June 30 Tuesday

Up at 6.30. Had a good night. Prayer meeting. On duty in tent. Meeting at 11.0. Afternoon meeting Dr Bickerton.

Out for Open air meeting. Much conviction but no open results. Felt a great desire to stop and try to lead them to happiness. Fine time at night—Principal, good crowd and about 50 out after Mr Dunning's appeal.

July 1 Wednesday

Fine Prayer Meeting—(no singing) Dr & his wife led, they are fine—had a real blessing—? spoke at Breakfast, also H May and Jones Jackson was fine for Cliff men. 11.0 Principal on Perfection. Afternoon two missionaries—CIM & JEB. Missionary tea. (got wheel repaired 8/6). Evening Mr H May & Davies—a long meeting and a good many results.

July 2 Thursday

P. M—Mr Lambert & Mr Brice—in real Prayer—a blessing. Dr Bick at Breakfast—Keep True (6d to pay Mr Eden—paid short).

July 3 Friday

Southport–Liverpool 22 miles. 7.0 Prayer Meeting. 8.0 Trekker's Meeting.

All treks start but only one goes on—others return and have breakfast—we tidy up and get off. 6 miles then dinner (water free) on to Liverpool app 14 miles—rain and sets. Tea at a Teashop—No Bill Praise God.

To boat and get aboard by 9.30 and off at 10.30.

To bed on lower deck—lent blanket. Middle deck with men and women piled all over. Not sea sick.

July 4 Saturday Belfast

"Up" at 4.0 and washed. On deck but not sea sick—rather surprised—seen I. O. M. Photo. Off boat 8.15.

Open air at Bangor, sent by minister, a very fine place on Belfast Loch. Open air at Belfast.

July 5 Sunday

10.15 Morning Sunday School—app 10 c.11.0 Service—good time. dinner.

2.15 Primary SS Bro Guest & I—good time. Great open air on the Custom House steps—Tea—Prayer meeting.

7.0 service. Testimony in large hall —app 1500 people there four or five dec.

9.00 open air after Lords supper—good atmosphere but no open dec. —and so to bed

(Sisters Blair, Cathcart & two others very good to us.)

11.55

July 6 Monday—26 miles

Late start from Grosvenor Hall. Bro Brown & me. Through Lisburn–Moira–Lurgan—Bro Savery left the trek (good place for dinner, free, W&M) rain on the way and concrete road. Bro Brown & Guest drop out & Bro Holmes rides Bro Fees cycle. Very tired when we get to Portadown—tea at Cafe. March round about 2 mls with Bro Hudson.

Open Air—good crowd—conviction but no open results—people very shy of coming out but very reverent and attentive—good supper & to bed at 11.45.

July 7 Tuesday 26 miles

From Portadown—Bro Guest rides 5 mls. Bro Brown rides all the way except 4 miles on cart, milk float, lorry and m/c. Bro Holmes runs ahead and struggles on before us—good dinner in barn & on again to Antrim—stay in Antrim Dormain near castle—tea at minister's—open air and Bro Fullerton arrives to tea. Bro Fullerton visits the barber with good results.

To bed—ghost laid—good night—up and doing at 7.45.

July 8 Wednesday 10 miles

7. 45 Left Antrim & Lock Neagh to place for dinner 4 miles on—man interested but will 'think';—open air at mill.

On to Ballymena. No tea ready so have to start and get ready—Minister comes in—sorry—a good chap—a very good open air—fine crowd. Other demonstration of Orange men only appeared to help us. 2 men come in for sanctification & so to bed on landing with Bro Hand, Bro Holmes & Fergeson disturb

---

July 9 Thursday 20 miles

To Temperance Hotel for Breakfast—good feed—off for Larne—up hill nearly all the way for 15 miles.

Bro Brown in by Ford car. Tea to get ready & wash up then open air—difficult time. Miss Blair & other came over for a few mins—drunk interrupts but crowd are shy. cart to cost 38/- tomorrow—money? & so to bed on SS platform.

July 10 Friday 17 miles

Left Larne—10.0—cart cost 4/6. By SS Margaret LMS—39 mls over to Stranraer Harbour. Cart out and away at 1.0 for dinner outside town—sausages cooked with drift wood—forced march on to Ballantrae—17 leaving at 3.0 & arriving at 8.40. Open air meeting—people very shy. To supper on bread and jam. Only 1/- left in trek fund & £1 in debt. Slept on garage floor.

July 11 Saturday 13 miles

Ballantrae to Girvan. Good breakfast—eggs given by minister of Presby church. Off on way along coast in sight of Ailsa Craig out at sea. Fine country on coast road. Stop for dinner by road side—drift wood fire—heavy rain & so on to Girvan good place—tea—O A no one to listen so stir them up with the cart— Bro H, Fullerton & I and then try again—poor do until Pierots leave—Bro Devon & I have a "chat" & people gather round—120 or more adults & 70-80 children—a great time but no open results at first. 2 children later. Bag of apples given.

July 12 Sunday

Good breakfast—service at 11.30—Mr Brisco. Dinner at Mr W Girvens, 8 Henrieta St Girvan. Service in little Mission Hall—not open air—disappointed. Tea at Girvens—very kind Scots. Service—2 min testimonies. open air, a crowd of 120 adults, 70 children no decision. Money given—sufficient to cover the debt and leave a bit over. Supper & bath & so for doxology & to bed 11.30 pm.

3 pots jam—1 cake—candles—box kippers—pan—3 bags apples—pkt cakes—tin milk—beans—peaches—tin biscuits— glass tongue—milk—cheese.

July 13 Monday 22 miles

Girvan to Ayr. Stayed in barn for dinner. On again—no place in town arranged. A man came up after we had asked for first one place and then another and not found a place, and asked us if we were seeking a place—which he was vainly 'thinking' of a place, another man a friend of his came up and told us we could have Mill St Hall. Open air meeting a great time and three souls. (Two men 'sent' to give us a shelter, one came another followed.) Crowd of 200 odd & children. Praise God 3 converts—open. 6/- given me—in small.

July 14 Tuesday 18 miles

Ayr to Stevenston. Leave the children etc. with a song. Someone gives us cakes etc. & another bread—stayed at house for dinner in a greenhouse—Bro Holmes off. Tea at the minister's house. Rain. Open air meeting at the level crossing. Supper & so to bed.

July 15 Wednesday 25 miles

Stevenston to Paisley. Up early to write to Edith, off at 9.0, via Kilwinning—Beith. Dinner & then rain again. A long tramp—tired—tea at the cafe with minister. Open air in a little park and then the rain comes down & spoils it. Young man in—a talk—he got through OK. To bed.

July 16 Thursday

Paisley. Open air at 12–1.0 a good crowd and interest—did not testify. Lunch at Cafe, a good do—to the Park for aft out. Tea & children's service. 8.0 meeting in lower hall 12–15 decisions. A very good meeting.

July 17 Friday 5 miles

Breakfast at the minister's house—nieces request a very nice home—visited Abbey. Written home, sent undervest. Bro Hudson gets young painter converted in abbey. Off to Glasgow at 2.25 Partick. Open air—2 converts. Drunks round & other meeting started. The whistler—you are inclined to make me laugh! (Remember what your mother used to say to hens.)

July 18 Saturday 6 miles?

To (Gallowgate) Bridgeton Wesley Hall. Lunch in Glasgow Green. Tea at Cafe—a good 'High Tea' eggs, fish etc.

Open air meeting 7.30. Drunks again—we are in worst part of Glasgow (12.15pm drunks)young men drunk in streets. Very good meeting but drunk answers appeal & we close.

July 19 Sunday

11.30 meeting Bro Fullerton & I testify—Bro Hudson preaches. Good service & one convert. Dinner—real Sunday dinner. SS Primary—Bro G & I good time. To ministers to tea. Evening service—very good meeting. Bro Devonshire preached—open air—a good meeting one open decision—for deeper experience, 2 men later, Bro Hu.

July 20 Monday 15 miles

Bridgeton to Kilsyth (1st dry town). Minister—Rev Steuart—good tea ready for us. Open air, fair crowd, Mr Lambert joins trek. To supper out.

July 21 Tuesday 15 miles

Kilsyth—Stirling on river. Good trek—quick work too. Bro Fullerton off—for day, not well. Mr L with us. Tea ready for us. Seen Bannockburn on way also Stirling Castle. Rain. Open air Friargate—about 5 converts—good time. Stopped having a late meeting.

July 22 Wednesday 20 miles

Stirling—Auchterader. Photo of Wallace's Memorial. Very fine view of Stirling. To Evangelistic Hall. To tent meeting in rain & short open air after.

July 23 Thursday 14 miles

Auchterader to Perth. Good day and only a shower at noon—over the Earn bridge. Two open airs 7.0–10.0.

July 24 Friday 15 miles

Perth–Blairgowerie. Bros Holmes & Devonshire leave us. Cook now. Saw famous hedge of beech trees.

July 25 Saturday 19 miles

Blairgowerie–Dundee. Leave in rain. Very heavy rain to Coupar Angus—stop for shelter & the Lord sends a dinner.

14 miles over big hills after lunch—arrive a bit wet at Dundee—tea ready for us. Tent meeting, great power & results.

July 26 Sunday

Dundee. Mr Lambert preaches on sanctification. Out at a big Hotel for lunch—great feed. To Girls Industrial School with Bro H a real good time but wet through—for tea a nice house—back to church & get changed—Mr Lambert gives address many are convicted but no open results. A great prayer meeting—wonderful time & great power.

A pot of jam—jar to be returned.

This PM started the Real Work of the Trek.

July 27 Monday

Dundee to Newport. Went to Broughty Sands and had open air. Lunch with Miss Douglas's sister. Over on ferry to Newport—open air at Tayport. Tea at Mr Robert's. Open air 30 adults round. Young men too a talk with 4 of them in hall with them & joy in getting them to make a decision—all got through OK. One a scout. Sing Song in Mr Roberts' house.

—————————————————————————

July 28 Tuesday 30 miles—lorry

Newport–Milnathort. Up early—breakfast and off in lorry. One of young men came to see us off. Letter from E at Cupar. 'Continuing' minister Mr Combe very kind to us—putting. Meeting in village & at Kinross. Mr Lambert left.

—————————————————————————

July 29 Wednesday 27 miles

Milnathort–Falkirk. By Rumbling Bridge and to Kincardine Ferry—only a small boat—goat at dinner—rain. Bro G went in bus at finish and so only four of us to pull. 4 converts in indoor meeting. 2 converts in outdoor meeting. Good time & welcomed—next year. Minister Rev Thompson married at Helperby. Young man came right out before we sang.

—————————————————————————

July 30 Thursday 20 miles

Falkirk—Coatbridge. Railway Mission. Good ground near the fountain, nearly all men—'I'm that scotch sausage!' Some children came after Bro H. stayed. Very near the trains all night.

July 31 Friday 14 miles

Coatbridge–Armadale. Tea with minister. Shaft of cart to renew. Open air—good time. 3 young men came right out. Two before we sang—one a RC. Young lady and children later.

August 1 Saturday 20miles

Armadale–Edinburgh. Forced march for time. Happy rope taken off for mile or two, good fun. To Faith Mission Conference at Edin—tea and testimony (£2.2). To Abbey Hill Railway Mission & to open air—drunk becomes violent while I am speaking and breaks things up a bit but we get to prayer and a woman comes out. Praise God.

Why should Archbishop have £40 a week?

August 2 Sunday

To Mr Stewart's for breakfast. To Central Hall for service. Mr Benson very good meeting 'Rejoice rather' Mt 10:20.

To Park for open air in aft (written home)—two came out in the park. Open air at 6.30-7.0 then service in Mission—no open results. Off by car to West End open air. Soon have a great crowd but have to close 9.30 and no open results. Hundreds of people in Princes St.

August 3 Monday 23 miles

Breakfast at Stewarts. Off to Peebles at 9.30. Bank Holiday. Very quiet town. Tea ready at Rly Mission—OA none stood round. To bed early.

August 4 Tuesday 18 miles

Peebles–Galashiels. Through Tweed valley, very good run, bath in River. Bros F & Hn left behind. Tea ready for us. Halliburton Mission House. Hair cut 8d. Three open air.

August 5 Wednesday 25–6 miles

Galashiels–Duns. Good Breakfast and off at 9.30. Seen Melrose Abbey over valley. Very Hilly journey. Feet skinned a bit. Tea with Mrs Dixon 16 The Mount Easter Rd—Faith Mission people. Open air—good witness—no near crowd. Slept in FM hall.

August 6 Thursday 15 miles

Duns–Berwick on Tweed. To Mission Hall. Tea with Missioner. Crossed the border today back in old England. Photo of Border. Open air in street, then service in Hall. Pastor Wallace—Wallace Green Mission Hall. Two boys & SM drowned. Bro H late in from Kelso.

August 7 Friday 14 miles

Berwick–Belford. Bambro Castle & Holy Island seen from road.

Called at Mr Youngs Baker. To PM chapel—stove on the go. No convenience whatever. Open air—good time but crowd shy.

August 8 Saturday 15 miles

Belford–Alnwick. Rain on way. Bro Fullerton left his bag at noon. Over Lion Bridge & by castle in Alnwick. Very cold so cannot stay out long in open air, not much doing.

August 9 Sunday

Hear young man trial sermon for note. To Mr Bambridge for dinner etc. Open air in market—cold in afternoon. On 5. 5 bus to Felton for evening service—invite in—19 there— good time. Back on 9.45 bus—open air but not much crowd. 2 picture houses open on Sunday. Food and Money.

August 10 Monday 8 miles

To Amble. We amble along. Dinner on way, in early. Tea prepared for us. Open air at top of Queen St. Good crowd round but no open results. Sing Song & to bed in school.

August 11 Tuesday 11 miles

Amble to North Seaton. Colliery village where Bro Devonshire had a mission. Bad road into village but a warm welcome at Mr & Mrs Stewart's caretaker of school for tea with Bro Henderson—they know & love PTH(utchison). Others speak well of him. Meeting at 6.0 inside. Good time. Open air after—great time many stand round—we speak from a wheel barrow and as appeal is made a young woman comes and shakes Bro D's hand and then falls on her knees on the footpath where we are knelt—no coat etc. Mrs Steward leads her to Christ—another young woman who takes fits cried Lord have mercy and is carried out and so meeting has to close. Praise God for a real powerful witness.

August 12 Wednesday 16 miles

N Seaton to North Shields. Dinner near Blyth Harbour. Mr Stewart brings Bro Hn. Tea at Coach Lane Church. Open air in Stevenson St. Four young ladies and some men came out after service.

August 13 Thursday 3 miles

Did not leave for Rose Hill until late. Dinner in grub shop. 1 convert in open air at Rose Hill, 8 at Wallsend. Conservative speaker on same ground—very good place— supper with Spood. Friars—they must work for eggs and bacon.

_._

August 14 Friday 6 miles

Rose Hill–Snow Street. Children's Meeting—out singing and girl brings a penny. My first attempt at start singing— one convert in OA.

_._

August 15 Saturday

Mother & Dad over. Out to dinner at Mrs Glover. Service at Mt. OA. Plenty of children at Children's Service.

_._

August 16 Sunday

Bro F gave address at 10. 45. Children at 2.30 & 5.30 & adults at 6.30. Good time and good crowd but no open results until after service, then about 1–2. Out to dinner so could not get away to Central Station for 1.20.

_._

August 17 Monday 11 miles

Snow St–Great Lumley. Stop for dinner given by a friend. Service in Church & then OA. Young man came later through happy. Praise God.

_._

August 18 Tuesday 7 miles

Great Lumley–Sacriston (photo taken on way). To tea and all meals to Mr Tate. Sacriston—Durham. Open air meeting at 7.30, a good crowd and again at 10.0. Men very interested.

August 19 Wednesday

Meeting at 11.0—Prayer & address. Meeting indoors at 2.30. Great power but no appeal made. Meeting indoors at 7.30. Great time & full house. 2 or 3 converts but did not get them out. 10.0 open air great crowd & great atmosphere but no open results and so to bed after taking home a man called Robson promised to see me at W. E.

August 20 Thursday 9 miles

Sacriston–W Cornforth. Prayer meeting 10. –10.30. Good bye to good friend. Through Durham—saw cathedral. Open air then into PM Church. Good meeting & full do. Open air again & out to supper. No open results.

August 21 Friday 5 miles

W Cornforth–Windleston. Meeting in chapel, very nice chapel. To tea at Mr Welch's school teacher & supper— open air later. No open results among adults.

August 22 Saturday 12 miles

Windleston–Edmondsley. OA indoor meeting and open air. Happy get some later.

August 23 Sunday

10.30 address Jn 7:37. 2.0 SS. 6.0 good service. Converts and app 30 for S. Good open air later. To Atkinsons for supper.

August 24 Monday 12 miles
Edmondsley–Spennymoor. To dentist's then OA and on to Tent. Spoke in tent. Wm MacEwan singing. Full tent & a Hell Fire preacher but not open results. To supper with Bro S Bakewell.

_ _ . _ . . _ . _ . . _ . _ . . _ . _ . . _ . _ . . _ . _ . . _ . _ . . _

August 25 Tuesday 9 miles
Spennymore–Howden le Weir. Children's meeting 6.0. Out with Ch for an invitation round. Bro Devonshire stayed at Spennymore. Good OA Young Chadwick spoke.

_ _ . _ . . _ . _ . . _ . _ . . _ . _ . . _ . _ . . _ . _ . . _ . _ . . _

August 26 Wednesday 15 miles
Howden le Weir to Consett. Heavy road and warm day. Tea got ready for us. Good crowd in OA but no open response.

_ _ . _ . . _ . _ . . _ . _ . . _ . _ . . _ . _ . . _ . _ . . _ . _ . . _

August 27 Thursday 3 miles
Consett–Ebchester. Open air in market place at 10.30, over 100 around and a good time. Meeting inside. 30 stood for fuller commitment. Open air—to Garage for supper & oil.

_ _ . _ . . _ . _ . . _ . _ . . _ . _ . . _ . _ . . _ . _ . . _ . _ . . _

August 28 Friday 9 miles
Ebchester–Ryton. One spoke gone on way. In garden for dinner. Tea ready for us. Very good open air at the place Wesley spoke at.

_ _ . _ . . _ . _ . . _ . _ . . _ . _ . . _ . _ . . _ . _ . . _ . _ . . _

August 29 Saturday 6 miles
Ryton–Newcastle. To Elswick port. Back Leadman St Gospel Hall. Good indoor welcome meeting. Two converts

and a number for full salvation. Open air good meeting but
ends in a row among the drunks.

August 30 Sunday

Morning Prayer Meeting and service. Out to dinner at Mr
Bowmans. Children's service 2.30. Open air 6.0. Service at
6.30. Good company and great power at the very end.
About 18 converts praise God. Open air in Cannon St, good
hearing and so to bed.

August 31 Monday

To town in morning. Out to dinner again. Sisterhood at
2.30, good time. Children's service at 6.0 full do, about 15
out. Good meeting at night. 4 converts and 2 come for full
salvation.

September 1 Tuesday

To People's Hall, Gateshead. No preparation for us. Rain
and short open air. Helped with indoor service.

September 2 Wednesday

Rain again. Noon service in town two converts—men.
Evening Service. One out for sanctification & one witness.

September 3 Thursday

To Vineyard in Vine St. Helped in tent with evening
service—results. Met Bro Day; a trophy of Grace & Sister
Winifred, a saintly soul.

September 4 Friday

Morning meeting at 11.0. (Got my ref back from Cleethorpes.) Mr Lambert came at night and gave address. Good number of converts.

September 5 Saturday

Gave address at 11.0 on Rom 12:1, faith. Tea in afternoon and then Parade round. Bro Hudson gave address in tent Mr Turner over to see us. Good time & a number of results.

September 6 Sunday

Gave address on John 7:37 in Vineyard to good congregation. Good time. In SS at 2.30 to 3.30. Slow. Evening Service for Children at 5.30. Adults 6.30 Bro Devonshire. No open results. To tent Mr Howe on two converts. Got cold.

September 7 Monday

Bro Devonshire at Prudhoe St. 16 women decided out of the 580. Praise God. Children in tent—open air very good time with children singing. In tent converts—an old lady, a middle aged lady in black, a young.

September 8 Tuesday 2 miles

Vine St to Prudhoe St Newcastle. To G Bowman's mission. Met Sister Jenny. Great meeting in hall. People there from Snow St, Back Loadmana. St Peoples Hall, Vine St and Chstoke St. Mr Sloan over and got my address. Three hands up—men great time, about 550 there.

September 9 Wednesday

'Telephone'. Evening Prayer Meeting at 6.30. Open air in big market, 7 converts. One man 61 years old Confirmed and baptised. Promised to write to him. Praise God.

September 10 Thursday 2 miles

PM From Prudhoe St to Wolsey Road. To mission Hall for dinner by car. Hard meeting one out for Full Salvation.

YP out for salvation. Tongues people.

September 11 Friday

To Jesmond Dene. Children's Service. Good meeting indoors. Lady and baby out for salvation, young lady out.

September 12 Saturday 29 miles

Newcastle–W Auckland. Bro Hudson gone home. Left at 9.0. Met man from Edinburgh at Birley—stop for dinner at Hall's. To West Auckland at 5. 45, tired—only four of us. Open air and indoor service good times but no open results.

September 13 Sunday

At service in morning at Wesleyan Methodist and Prayer meeting. Out to Mr Alderson's for dinner. To PM for afternoon service Jn 7:37. Also at night—good time and 110 there. No open result. Good after meeting and open air. One soul at WM and young people in SS. To Mr Wilson's for supper and so to bed.

September 14 Monday 19 miles

No letter. West Auckland to Catterick. Helped out of village and gave tract. Shave at noon. Tea with Miss Morrell's and supper too. Bro D to Catterick Camp, 7 decisions. Bro H and I held meeting in chapel. Mother and Miss U over with Uncle George.

September 15 Tuesday 12 miles
Catterick to Northallerton. Breakfast at Miss Morrell's. Hot day for tramp. Bro Sunley's young lady came out in open air. Praise God. Good time at Northallerton.

September 16 Wednesday 9 miles
Northallerton–Thirsk. Good open air at Thirsk. No open result. Bro Sunley joined.

September 17 Thursday 14 miles
Thirsk–Borobridge via Pilmoor. At home for dinner. Good crowd at Borobridge. Two converts. Dad and Norman there.

September 18 Friday 10 miles
Borobridge–Harrogate. In for dinner at 29—good to be there again. Praise God. Half day off. For walk with Bro F.
Indoor meeting at 7.30, good company, and good time. Open air at 8.30, good time & 6 converts. Praise God.
Supper at 29 and so to bed. Bro Holmes over.

September 19 Saturday 18 miles
Harrogate–Leeds. Via Harewood. Tea at Arms. Norman with us for dinner. Rain later, got to Holbeck—Mayne St—wrong place—7.30 indoor meeting. 9.45 open air 'drunks meeting'.

September 20 Sunday

Morning service—scouts parade. Afternoon SS some good decisions. Bible Class, good company. Evening appeal not answered. PM hard time.

— · — · — · — · — · — · — · — · — · — · — · — · — · — · —

September 21 Monday 49 miles

Up early and away for Hemmingfield at 8.40 via Wakefield—dinner at Mellors. New Miller dam—met trek 1.

To Hemmingfield at 4.45. Tea and shout round meeting at 7.30, supper and off again. Both teams at 11.0 to Sheffield about 1.0 over water splash and rough road.

Tuesday into Cliff tired out at 6.45 a.m.

Praise God for a great Trek.

Chapter 8

Evangelist

But College days ended and my 'faith' was to be put to the test straight away for I returned home with no job prospects. I had put my name down with Cliff as an evangelist but had heard nothing.

To take up the diary at the end of the Trek, Norman arranged for me to join him at Staithes. I was to cycle and getting to Borrowby the free wheel broke down and I peddled without making progress. I took it to pieces and inserted a bit of wood where the spring should have been and proceeded with a fixed wheel for the rest of the journey. Norman must have had a car by this time and would bring me home.

On Oct. 16th., I had a telegram saying 'Prepare to travel Dunstable tomorrow'. A letter came next morning and I left for Cliff Missions. I had put my name down and nothing had come my way until this. There had been a mistake in the office and I should have joined Brother Skinner earlier, he proceeded with the meetings he had already begun in a P.B. Hall. Adult and children's meetings went well and we had a good home base. They lent us their car for a trip to Whipsnade Zoo on our day off. I note that 17 made confession of faith.

A Cliff Mission involved taking services every evening, preaching on alternate days and sharing the Sunday services. Doing some visiting in an attempt to get new people in to the meetings. Much depended on the prayerful attitude of the church. Dunstable was a good start and we had another local effort and then moved on to the border of Wales Oct. 31st.

Here we were in the heart of the country so very different from a mission in town. I note that our first was in a farm kitchen and when it filled up people sat on the stairs. Conditions were primitive and when we found a crease in the bedside rug we lifted it up and found the rat hole. The animal had visited us in the night hence the crease! On the next farm Bro. S. went ahead to preach an the Sunday while I did the last Sunday at the old one. When I joined him he said 'The place is haunted' I believe it was called 'Hangman's Farm'. It had a wide hall with a sort of gallery at upper floor. Bro. S was a townie and that night I was able to confirm that the 'haunting' was rats racing across the rafters over our heads. It was at this farm we were provided with horses on which to go visiting. I got back ache as I was not used to such travel.

To my surprise I note that I did sing some solos during these missions. We crossed the border to Clun and had a mission in Ludlow. I note that one man followed up our visit to his church - he cycled 14 miles and said when we greeted him that he had come to get converted. On one occasion I note a bus load came and we had a full chapel. How much we depended on the prayers of new students and the readers of the Cliff paper 'Joyful News' we shall never know but we did have a fair number of professed conversions. During one mission we had a day off and were loaned shot guns to join the farmer rabbiting. I fear we were not good shots and Bro. Skinner less used to guns then me peppered a worker's lad with shot. He was not badly hurt but it might have been serious, the following day Bro. S went again but I refused for I was shocked at the possible consequences we had missed.

It was at this time I had the letter from Mr W. Boddy asking if I would be the Missioner at Starbeck Railway Mission.

Home for Christmas Dec. 22nd full of praise for what God had done during Cliff Missions. My diary has helped me again here as I had forgotten that we had one more Mission in the new year.

I am surprised at the intensity of my activities just then. It reads like this—Home 22nd. Dec. Address at Watch Night Service in Harrogate Town Mission 31st. spoke from 1 Cor. 6 v19/20 'Our body a temple of the Holy Spirit.'

1932 3rd Jan. preached at Dishforth and Norton-le-clay. With Uncle to Thirsk and Bedale and on to see Grandad at Burrill. 4th. home on cycle 5th. to Harrogate on 7th. and to see Mr Boddy at Starbeck, 8th to Leeds to get photo and a 50/- suit! It is worthy of note that at Cliff we were wearing khaki shirts and slacks with a jacket with Cliff Badge for use on Sundays etc. I did not have a suit. 9th Home with Edith, 10th preached twice at Helperby (next village to home), 11th to Thirsk (old job friends), 12th to see Mr & Mrs Ireland (old S.S. teacher), 13th to Harrogate, 14th home again, 15th to Harrogate & Open Air Meeting, 16th left for my final Cliff Mission at Leintwardine (16th to 25th.) Preaching alternate nights we ended our 10 day Missions with a 'Faith Tea'—it was open for folk to bring whatever they liked—then a lecture on the Cliff Trek. Jan 29th back to Harrogate, 30th got lodgings at 41 The Avenue, Starbeck, and attended the first funeral ever of anyone known to me and returned to Pilmoor. Sunday at Sessay for the service, Monday 1st. Feb. started at Starbeck.

It is impossible to know the true value of a Cliff Mission but during our missions we indicated that 43 adults had made confession of faith. We preached for open results and each night I wrote N.O.R. in my diary if there had been no open result. It was a habit I continued at Starbeck for some time.

Looking back over the years I marvel at the great grace of God who saw fit to use such a one as me and at the many many helps I had on my way. Mother did my washing by post and there was always an open house for me and every encouragement from Edith's parents at Harrogate.

Chapter 9

Railway Missionary

During the Cliff Missions I had a letter which was really to start me on my life's work.

It was from the Railway Mission at Starbeck near Harrogate who were prepared to appoint me without my even having to appear before the Committee or to 'preach with a view'. I was just 21 years of age, (February 1932).

It would seem that both our families had a long association with the Mission. Mother and Dad had lived in Starbeck and one of my early recollections is of our attending the Anniversary meetings, being with a crowd of older people and returning to Pilmoor on the late Saturday night train, half asleep. Edith's father helped to run a men's club in Starbeck and mother used to tease him about the fact that she saw him leave work and return to the club so quickly that she said his sisters must have been waiting on him. He used to say that he had six sisters and each one had a brother. It is with this background that I try to explain how I came to be invited to become their Missionary. I do not recall having given an address at the Mission, though I may have done so, certainly I had given an address at the Harrogate Town Mission but there was no connection. I had a letter from mother while on Cliff Missions mentioning the possibility, but it now seems absurd that I saw no committee and did not 'preach with a view', gave no references and as far as I know Cliff was not contacted. I just had a letter while on Cliff Missions from Mr William Boddy asking me to become their leader. I agreed and just saw Mr Boddy briefly before my first Sunday.

I accompanied Mr Boddy, a retired railwayman, to the Prayer meeting that first Sunday morning and as we walked down the side of the old Mission Hall to the side vestry he explained that the garden area was intended for a Sunday school hall. That was on Sunday 7th Feb. 1932. There had been 43 at the Welcome Meeting the previous Thursday.

Decision to have a School Hall was taken at a Full Committee composed of the local (Starbeck) committee and the Harrogate Committee. I note that there was £90.00 in hand towards that project. I note that I met the builder, a Mr Kitchen, on the 29th. Under God that was a vital contact, he was a Methodist and I feel sure he put the project through at cost price.

I note that I was able to pay for Edith's cycle by the 7th. March. For the first time I had a 'living' wage of £2-3-5 per week and a modest charge for accommodation with a motherly Methodist lady.

We had a Prayer meeting at 9.30 on Sunday, a 3 o'clock devotional meeting and the evening service. Sunday School used the same hall and a Bible Class used the vestry. Some time later we met at 11 o'clock. With March I again saw Mr Kitchen so progress was being made with plans etc. On March 31st we had a public meeting re the New Hall. The chairman of the Harrogate Committee was a Mr D. G. Browne who had big furniture and general store in town. He too must have been a vital part of the team, and later he was most kind to us with all we needed to set up a home at 'trade price'.

There was a prayer meeting on Tuesday evening and I note we had 17. In April I note that I visited the Public houses with the 'Railway Signal' papers giving away 30 copies. The attendance on Sunday evening had risen to 70 by May. That month I attended the May Meetings of the Railway Mission in London staying one night there. I had a Pass to cover Harrogate, Starbeck and Knaresborough and a free pass for the London visit.

I had my first funeral at that time and went to get advice from Mr Govier, the Town Missionary. He was always helpful.

After my Cliff experiences I had an unshakeable faith in God and in a very simple way I was assured that the money for the building would come in time. One committee rather shocked me with their worldly-wise discussion of how to secure a loan to pay the builder. God was in the project from the word go. On May 25th. we had the stonelaying of the New hall; an old stone was also re-laid I believe. We opened the building free of debt on Aug. 20th. 1932.

I note that 'bricks' and donations brought in £139.16, Tea £5.16.8½ Offering £1.10.10½ bringing the total in hand to £367.7.4. There was a little over to pay for some equipment and of course it transformed the work of the Mission and its Sunday School. I cannot quite remember the final figure but it was less than £600. I rather think it was about £550—tribute to the builder. It must be remembered that this was a very considerable sum for those people at that time. A Mrs Harrison gave very generously in response to my appeal.

At that time I learned from HQ it would be in order to have a Communion Service.

In June a Full Committee agreed to my appointment for three years D.V. We could have a communion rail and we could circulate people re a change to a morning meeting. Miss

Jackson paid for the rail and kneeler. I note that I asked for a "Penitent Form" (like the Salvation Army).

After 19 weeks I noted that the average offering was £1.3.3¼. Visits to homes 280, visits to men 40, addresses 57, average congregation 60.

Christmas Day fell on a Sunday that year and I had hoped for a big day but was disappointed. Some of the 'faithful office bearers' failed to attend.

Incidentally I had a holiday in Staithes after the Opening of the hall. Edith going with me but recalled as her mother was unwell. I always enjoyed visits to Staithes and that was no exception.

Life in Starbeck settled down to preaching twice on Sundays, a midweek Bible Study and Women's Meeting and a very well attended Prayer Meeting. I visited railwaymen at their work usually on Fridays and visited homes and anyone in hospital day by day.

The financial statement in the back of the diary is interesting, income each week seems to have been £2.3.5d and rental £1.5.7d. It looks so very odd now.

1933

Letters had gone up to 1½d but postcards were still 1d but printed papers ½d.

The new year began with a small attendance due to sickness but Edith's Aunt made a confession of faith at the Anniversary when Edith's father gave the morning address and a Mr Wood at night. Completing my first year I note approx. 124 addresses to adults and about 600 visits to homes.

I note I bought boots at the Co-op sale for 10/-. I preached twice at Topcliffe in Feb. and note that Edith sang well. I have no record of the date but by this time I had got permission to ask Edith to be my wife and had asked the committee if we could have the use of the Mission House which was let. Committees were postponed and Edith notes this delay in her diary, however on March 29th we got the necessary permission—I note 'we can get married and only pay rates'. My grandfather came with my mother to visit—it must have been quite a venture for him as he did not read or write. A Mrs Redfern gave me her old Yost typewriter—it had a pad for inking the type but started me off as a one finger typist.

From time to time I note that people made confession of faith. I still took the occasional Methodist service and note that I preached at Helperby (next village to Pilmoor) and my boyhood friend was there. Attended May Meeting of the Railway Mission. I noted that a lady named Elsie Wood made confession of faith—she was sister to George Wood. A Salvationist who had retired to Starbeck came forward one Sunday morning to kneel at the rail and find restoration. He was a very dear friend. My brother Norman was married in June, his bride being from Staithes. For Edith and I it was a busy time getting the house ready. I note with thanksgiving that Mr D. G. Browne had agreed to let us have furniture at a low rate. We set up house for less than one hundred pounds, I believe. A C. of E. lady gave us enough (£5) to book a week at Keswick Convention and we were married on July 15th. The Mission Choir sang 'God be with you till we meet again' on the station platform in Harrogate. We were only going away for two weeks and while we leaned out of the train window a porter got in at the other door and filled our cases with confetti. It was a great day with many gifts from family and friends.

Edith was not very well in Keswick but we enjoyed the ministry and then had the second week in Staithes.

It is worthy of note that Edith records being at Pilmoor working on Sarah Elizabeth's dress in May. I wonder how many wedding dresses she made in her life time. In July she mentions that she had the clock from Guides. She was by this time an officer. Years later that clock was stolen.

Of her wedding she notes "All went off splendidly" and we had the Canteen of Cutlery from the Mission.

Settled into the Mission House. Occasionally the next door neighbour had a phone call for me to go to hospital to give blood - early days of the service.

1933

During this year I started a Scout Troop in the Mission in an attempt to win boys for Christ. There was some superficial response but I doubt if there was the depth we required to establish a young men's group. It had been a year in which we held a special Mission and there had been professed conversions. The Sunday School doubled from about 60 to 120 over those early years once the Hall was open.

1934

The year began with my visit to a sale where I bought a piano for £8.15.0.

During this year we had a monthly meeting for Men and I appear to have taken an interest in a Y.P. Group in Harrogate which was to become the local branch of Young Life Campaign.

I visited Grandad for the day and note his words—"Keep pleading with the Master about those precious souls"!

I note in May that I was troubled and considering a possible move. Edith and I were both kept very busy but we saw little real growth. There is a long note in the diary "Not really happy these days" – "oh to be more useful and used, to be nothing yet filled" – regret that there had been no adult conversions in the year. Lack of unity was blamed. We were able to take a party to Cliff for the Anniversary on Whit Monday.

I seem to have had contact with the London City Mission over a number of years through their visits to Harrogate on deputation. I note I got a concertina from Mr George Pearce, the Deputation Secretary, and there is a very telling note in the diary for June, "Reading Hudson Taylor". Then later I resolved to seek out what the Lord had planned for me. "Paul said 'Lord What?' and the Lord showed him. While willing to leave all detail to His daily planning, I must seek His will for me more and more. Does he want me to be an Evangelist or a Pastor, or what? Lord give me a vision of my life work." In October the L.C.M. visit came round again and Mr Pearce said, "You ought to join us Mr T." "Having prayed that no door would open if we are to stay here, what does this mean? May I know the mind of the Lord!" It was clear I was seeking guidance with some urgency.

Having seen division caused by the traditional Sale of Work to raise funds I was able to persuade the Committee to have a Gift Day. Imagine my concern when it only brought in £17.9.6d. The following day I note "Edith waiting for me with the news of £50 from Mrs Harrison"—final total £66.18.0 clear. In November Miss Jackson the Harrogate Secretary sent for me and said it would be disastrous if I left. "May the Lord lead" is the note there. Almost at once I got a letter from Mr Pearce advising me to stay put until I had some clear guidance.

From time to time there is a note of a professed conversion of an adult. It was to be two years from that period of unrest before we left Starbeck.

1935

It seems that the Monthly Men's Meeting brought me much joy. In April we had a Cliff Mission in the Hall. Later in the year we had a visit from a Cliff Trek for two nights, and Y.L.C. appears so we had got Young Life Campaign going in Harrogate.

It is clear that we kept very busy but there is little comment in the diary for the year. A letter from Y.L.C indicates membership went up from 2 to 19 in the year.

1936

We appear to have issued cards for a Birthday Effort to raise funds and 31 were given out. That would indicate interest in the scheme to be limited. The shortage of funds was a constant concern and we could see no real future for us with such limited support.

Chapter 10

City Missionary

By the beginning of March I had evidently been in contact with the L. C. M as I was awaiting a letter. March 27th. I had a letter from L.C.M to go before the Committee. They sent me to Mr Kilbride, an ex-L.C.M, for his opinion. April 20th I saw a small Committee, then the whole Committee. I stayed nights with F. B. Robinson, Fire Brigade Missionary.

I saw the Mission Doctor and examiners on the 21st and others on 22nd and got home on the Pullman at 9.15. What a stressful time, yet I had peace. How Edith faced it all I shall never know, but she had a great trust. April 29th I had confirmation of acceptance. I note my fear of London and of a 'slums district' etc.

May 5th and 6th at Railway Mission Annual Meetings in London and stayed with members of Rye Lane Chapel in Coppleston Rd, Peckham. My first knowledge of Rye Lane Chapel. Little did I know what was to come. I had the opportunity to be at the Centenary Service of the L.C.M in St. Paul's. I was not yet a member but very pleased to be with them. At that time one of the founders of the Y. L. C. visited Harrogate for (I think) the first birthday celebrations.

Capt. J. C. Metcalfe visited us on the 21st May and so began years of very precious fellowship. Edith was well able to entertain all who came.

May 25th. I was distressed to hear I was to go to London as "a single man". How could I leave Edith, furniture in house and run two homes? This was resolved as I had lodgings with a dear old lady, Mrs Brooker, and was introduced to Northcott

Rd. Baptist Church. Furniture did stay in the house and Edith went home to her parents. I got paid my first salary after two weeks. Edith saw to the furniture being sent to London by rail when at last we were together. I said farewell to Starbeck on June 14th, was in London by 22nd and I had my official welcome to the L.C.M. on Oct. 5th.

We arrived in London with £13.12.0 between us. We were provided with a flat by the Mission, which was quite unusual in those days, but were required to pay rent. After having lived in Starbeck rent free this was quite a blow and we actually were 10/- a week worse off because of the move. It's quite amazing to me to think that Edith was prepared to leave home and face an uncertain life in London but it was an experience she was prepared to accept yet again many years later. She was always a better Christian than me.

I ran straight into trouble at the hall as the organist objected to choruses and asked that they be banned. Edith could play.

When we arrived in London we first attended the local Methodist church which was in the next street to the flat (near Clapham Common), but I regret to say that we were not given a very warm reception. Before our move I had lodged for a while as a probationer with a lady who was the widow of a former City Missioner. She was a member of Northcote Road Baptist Church in Battersea. So after our rather unhappy reception at the Methodist church, we transferred to the Baptist Church.

Long before we moved to London, Edith and I had desired to be baptised. Whilst in Harrogate we had not felt it appropriate to take this step but once in London the way opened up for us and a very dear friend of ours from the Railway Mission days, J. C. Metcalf, the Editor of the Overcomer undertook this ministry for us. Our subsequent move to the Baptist Church was thus not as random as it might have appeared at first sight.

And so we began our work in the Mission Church in Battersea to which we had been seconded. Edith immediately began a girls club and was privileged to lead some of them to Christ before I began to see any fruits in my own ministry. It was only a small Mission and I think there were only about 18 souls in all at our welcoming meeting. We were there for two years.

The fact that she could play was a great help to me in every way. We began to get children in and amid many difficulties we began to see blessing.

One amusing incident— we waited together for a bus to take us home. When it came I let the ladies get on first, like a gentleman, and then the bus went without me as it filled up. I learned a lesson in London life. It was at this time that J. C. , knowing I was very unhappy at Ridley Hall, contacted me to say a church wanted a Pastor. He must have believed that the 'Church would go through the Tribulation'—I'm glad I did not apply!

1937

I do not seem to have the diary for this year but my report to the Mission indicates that we were both working very hard to make known the gospel in a down town area.

I note that Edith had the senior girls' class in Sunday School and a mid week club with about 20 members doing sewing for Egypt General Mission work, games and a Bible Study. Some were led to Christ in that group. Edith took over the leadership of the Women's Meeting during that year. As we lived quite some distance from the hall, it called for real dedication on her part.

I seem to have had some success in door to door visiting as my report showed that some had responded to my visits in a positive way. We got the children to help us rub down the wooden benches and then we stained and varnished them, giving the Hall a cleaner appearance. The Hall Committee began to co-operate with us more and more though there was always a fear that we might 'take over' and it was their church.

1938

Increasing signs that war might come led me to offer for training with London Fire Brigade and I went for weekly training.

We had enjoyed a holiday during the previous year at Eastbourne Home and booked again for this year. The previous year we used our tandem to get about and we had some interesting trips in the London area on our day off. The year began well with a response on the part of a retired railwayman and his wife. He became a real helper. These were quickly followed by a young man and later his girl friend.

My treasured bicycle was stolen but I was helped to get another for £2.5.0. In March another member of the Johnson family was converted.

To our great joy it became clear that Edith was to have a baby but there was an ovarian cyst so she had an operation in

South London Hospital for Women. She came home an 16th May. Our miracle baby was safe.

War clouds gathered but we went to Eastbourne on holiday on June 17th, Hilda and May staying in the town. Edith was not very well but we had a good holiday and noted that we had both gained a bit in weight. Rye Lane Chapel now came into the picture as I note I was to see Mr Bamber on July 12th. and also had details of a possible dwelling. The house was far from the district and I turned it down.

Chapter 11

Rye Lane

Becoming a member of a Baptist Church was a very important step even though we did not know it at the time. We were very happy there—a lovely pastor and very happy fellowship. Sunday mornings we would meet with them before going in the afternoon to the Mission Hall. Headquarters did not favour their Missionaries changing denominations but I think that our District Secretary must have learnt of it from the reports which I despatched to him for I was duly asked by Headquarters to go and attend an interview with Rev T M Bamber in Peckham. The Rye Lane Baptist Church at that time seated 900 people but there were over 1100 names on the roll all having been baptised as believers. In addition to the main building it also had two mission halls attached to it. I am happy to say that Mr Bamber accepted me to be responsible for one of the Mission Halls, which was near the Old Kent Road.

James Grove Hall was my booking for July 17th. We were met at the Station and walked to the hall then walked to a tram. Edith was very tired. On July 26th I was instructed to begin in Peckham on Sept. 4th. At my farewell meeting at Ridley Hall there were 38 people, just 20 more than my first meeting I believe.

Mr Bamber always said that on that first visit it was not him that interviewed me but rather the other way round! Such perhaps is the arrogance of youth. It was a great joy to share in the morning service in a packed church under such a gifted teacher and preacher and to spend the rest of the day in 'our

Hall'. There had been constant friction between the mission and the parent church over the years in Peckham but I saw the vision of an effective mission connected with a live church and by the grace of God any division was healed completely.

At my welcome meeting at James Grove (North Peckham) there were 130 and I noted that the following day there were 18 at the prayer meeting and that 10 were men and at the Fellowship meeting there were 42. One of the Keeble brothers (Leslie) had his farewell after furlough soon after, and so began a family friendship that lasted years.

It was a thriving mission in many ways. It was open seven days a week and I think there was something going on every day or night. There were well over 100 women attending the women's meeting and some 400 children on the roll. Edith and I began the scouts and cubs and it was such a success that we ended up having a waiting list and so started a second pack.

We had two prayer meetings a week and soon after I went to Peckham we began to see conversions and there was a steady stream of young people who became Church members and played an active part in the Church life.

Because of the war I was invited to become a Deacon. I would not have been so invited at my young age, they were usually men of mature years, but because some had left London a new arrangement had to be made and instead of being elected the deacons would invite others to join their numbers and ask the Church to subsequently endorse the appointment. I was a Deacon for 27 years which of course really set the relationship between Church and Mission on a very firm footing. But when Mr Bamber went to Australia and New Zealand on a preaching tour I was still only allowed to do the pastoral visiting work, not the preaching on a Sunday!

There were over 100 at the Women's Meeting anniversary. I cycled each day to do my visiting etc. and Edith went with me on the tram for Sundays but it involved her being alone a great deal.

On October 24th. I took the Women's Meeting at James Grove and phoned the hospital to learn that we had a SON. Edith was in a Nursing Home facing Wandsworth Common.

1939

The year began with a Rally at which I note 100-130 adults, and about 100 children. The Sunday evening attendance could be 80 or more. I soon took over the Band of Hope and turned it into Sunshine Hour for the Children. I note that Phyllis Irons came forward at one meeting and she still helps in North Peckham, as Mrs Stoneham (1994). Soon I rejoiced to see God at work in lives and confessions of faith. In April we had a brief holiday and I preached at Starbeck Mission. In June there is a note of an Outing for the children and there is a photo in the album of 'Grandad' Taylor who had been the leader and some of the group.

We had been required to leave Kyrle Road and find a new dwelling which proved difficult. However we had help and moved to 174 Choumert Rd. The rent was £1.7.6. per week so we were again 10/- worse off for the move. It was quite a walk to the hall for Edith. David was dedicated at Rye Lane and Mrs Dean, a Deacon's wife, would wheel the pram to her home so that Edith was free to attend on occasion.

Miss Doris Green then let us have her house at 32 Cator Street (rent £1) and we moved there July 31st. There are photos of David in that garden too. We had some very happy days in Cator Street but war drew near and we had been issued with gas masks before we left Clapham Common.

On the 4th of August we left for holiday. I had made a carrier for David and there is a photo of him in it. So for 14 happy days we left the work and all thought of war. We returned home on Saturday Aug. 26th and just one week later Edith and David left for Harrogate and I was called up for service with the Auxiliary Fire Service on Friday 1st September. War was declared the following Sunday.

Children had been sent away to the country by train and life was now so very different. I note that the AFS paid me £2.18.5d for that first week. I note that I sent the pram and cot on the 15th. It was clear that we were to be parted for long periods.

Soon I had £3.0.0 from AFS plus 17/6 subsistence but we had to pay out from that. We worked for two days and nights and had one off, so I could keep in touch with the Mission Hall. The L.C.M. had advised us to take up war work, but I had long prepared for that to take place. I was able to pay a flying visit to Harrogate before Christmas.

I believe there were 7 children at the Sunday School that first week of all the crowd shown on the steps before the war.

Looking back at the diary, what a contrast. Jan. 1st 1939, about 60 at the brief service before we all went to Rye Lane Chapel for communion. Jan. 8th. a New Year Rally with 100 to 130 adults and about 100 children at the Mission. A similar number for the Sunday School Anniversary in March on the

Sunday and about 230 on the Tuesday. At the year end I spent Christmas day on duty with the AFS, most of the children had left London as had many adults. Yet there had been conversions that lasted.

1940

Jan. 4th I was able to leave the Fire Service full time (and go on duty one night in seven, I believe—or did that come later?)

Back in L.C.M. life went on much as usual, many children drifted back and I note attendance at the Sunday evening service was 60 to 80. Mid week Bible Study 30+ and I completed a study in Colossians after 14 weeks.

Edith and David and I had a holiday in Yorkshire in July and I took two services at the Railway Mission, Starbeck. Edith's mother and Dad and Hilda were with us late summer when a bomb fell in the city. Warnings increased all August until at the end of the month we had seven in a day. On Sept. 7th we went to see Mrs Brooker (widow of L.C.M with whom I had lodged). While there the warning went and as we returned home by tram we could see a big black cloud over dockland. When we got home I got into uniform and reported for duty with the AFS. There was only a taxi unit available (these were used to tow a small pump) and we were sent to the docks. I took over a pump and during the night the bombers returned, there was fire everywhere and little we could do. At last we were sent back to station and I went home to find that the school next to the Mission hall had been burnt out. During the night I had been 'given' a text— 'It shall not come nigh thee'—for the only time I had that assurance during the war. In view of the school we closed the Mission for the only time during the war (so I believe).

On the Tuesday night raid Alan Vallis, 14 year old son of one of the Mission workers was killed—drowned sheltering in the cellar. His father came to us in great distress and was put to bed. I told Edith to be ready to go. (I think she was always packed.) Mr & Mrs Bamber came to see Mr V. and it was then that I 'raided' our tithe box for the fare, and then received a gift of £2. Mr Bamber took us to the Underground and Edith and David left for Harrogate once more. Mr Vallis stayed with me and later George Drywood joined us and later still Harold Greaves, a school chum, came to get work and we lived together sleeping mainly in the Anderson Shelter in the garden. It is a sad commentary on social conditions that the boy's mother was not only distressed at the death of her son but cross with her husband that he had not retrieved the boy's new pullover!—Such was the effect of poverty.

1941

I note that I began the year with £4.1.3d in hand. It is interesting to note that we sent washing in a bag to a big laundry where all was washed in the bag and returned in same. Cost 1/9d to 2/- by weight—this was known as a Bag-wash!

Prices are unbelievable but Mr V. paid 15/- George 5/- on occasion and I allowed 10/- per week. Milk cost a surprising 2/-, rations 2/6, bread 5d, meat 1/10½ cake 4d, potatoes 6d, window glass and putty 2/4 due to bombing. About a dozen streets were affected by bombing and I visited casualties in hospital near Epsom where they were taken. On one occasion I visited 19 in one day. Many had nothing and L.C.M aid enabled me to provide books of stamps so they could write to friends. Glass splinters were left to 'grow out' so imagine what some looked like.

Following the Battle of Britain (Oct. 21st) bombing died down and Edith and David returned. Much changed. Young people found the evenings long after a 4.0 p.m. service, and I started an evening service on Sundays called the Fireside Fellowship. 40+ Adults joined us and we had some lively gatherings including some from another church.

We had a holiday in Yorkshire in July and I took the Sunday School Anniversary at Starbeck. I had been invited to become one of the 12 Deacons at Rye Lane Baptist Chapel—little did I know that I was to serve for 27½ yrs. On Nov. 19th we moved out of 32 Cator St (next Road to the Mission) to 98 Pepys Rd, New Cross near a park and a nice area. Mr & Mrs Metheringham were evacuated and offered us the ground floor in a big house. Cator Street had been much damaged—I believe there were 30 'incidents' within ½ a mile.

The Mission Hall suffered much and at times had tarpaulins on the upper floor so that we could use the lower hall.

1942

1942 began with a 4.15 'evening' service in the Mission and a 6.30 Fireside Fellowship. 37 at the first and 40 at the second. Later the service was at 6.0, but at 7.45 I record 60.

June saw us back in Starbeck on holiday and to preach. I also preached at Sessay and Helperby two villages nearest to Pilmoor. A Campaign at Rye Lane brought much blessing in July. Christian Endeavour played a big part in our work among young people and went on right through the war. I note that

Edith sang a solo at the Women's Own. In October I note that there were 32 young people at C. E. On October 18th we transferred the Fireside Fellowship to Rye Lane Chapel as it had grown to include so many from the parent church.

It seemed that most days were packed full and I marvel at the number of meetings that were fitted in. After some difficulty work was unified as Sunday School and Children's work ceased to be under parent church control and I became S. S. Supterintendent.

1943

Scouts now appear on the list and then Cubs run by Edith with help from a faithful convert of our early days and a dear friend, Vera Iveson. Edith had a cycle to get to meetings and I had made a saddle for David on mine with foot-rests—much appreciated.

On January 17th I note that there were 75 at the Fireside Fellowship held in Rye Lane Chapel School Hall. During the meeting the siren went and we obeyed the instructions of the Deacons that we were to go into the 'Strong Room'—a lower room specially strengthened with big beams.

The Young People continued to sing while I went to the door to await the 'All Clear'. What happened next I was not aware of but when I came to I was lying in the passage. It was for me the silent bomb of the war. A big High Explosive bomb had fallen on the local store Jones and Higgins across the road. The huge round window at the end of the School Hall (which had a gallery) had crashed on to the table where I had been sitting when the warning went. Rye Lane Chapel was devastated. When I went into the Strong Room all the Young folk were all right but the pianist was under the overturned piano. However she was unhurt. I had a cut head and that led to a joke of years later. The pianist, a Mrs Woodcraft, told me that she had found communion wine on her clothing when she got home. I did not tell her that it was a little of my blood! One lady whose light coat I marked in that way later charged me with its cleaning.

I cycled home to Pepys Road, then nearly passed out, but a nurse who shared the house put my head between my legs. A very unpleasant experience. I found then that I had a sprained ankle and had difficulty in walking. There was also shell-shock—for some time I could not hold a limb still when the warning went. I was off work for a couple of weeks.

Rye Lane members met in the Mission Hall on that following Sunday and then a local Methodist Church, not being used, was made available in Queens Road. It had to be cleaned by our members. I have a note on that sad Sunday when the chapel was wrecked—it just says 'Praise the Lord no Young People hurt. ' I still thank God for that.

In April I took a Sunday School Anniversary in Leicester. The Sunday School was growing again and we had 120 and a growing Bible Class.

In May there was a bomb in the Mission Road and 15 were killed and the hall damaged—a daylight raid when the barrage balloons were not up. In June the schooldays chum Harold was married to one of five sisters—all Christians, four being members of Rye Lane Chapel—named Allen. Another wedding dress I have no doubt.

I got the use of gardens of a bombed house and picked 112lb. of cherries from a big tree there.

By the end of August I note we had 12 fellows and 13 girls at Christian Endeavour as 'Double Summertime' ended. In September we began the Saturday Youth Club which was to bring in many Young People. Every night we had meetings of some sort. 'Blackout Meeting' started again that Autumn. A 'Make Do and Mend' class was begun. We got a catering licence for the Club. 20 cups of tea to one pint of milk etc.

1944

I had to go to Blackheath for the National Fire Service from February on. Again there were bombs on East Surrey Grove. Eleven were killed and 400 homes destroyed. Fifty families connected with the Mission. On the 25th I visited eighteen in the base hospital—some of them old scholars.

We had to leave Pepys Road and had accommodation at Muschamp Road again while owners were evacuated.

On June 6th I note 'Second Front opened'. Then while we had a Sunday School outing to Epsom Downs there was a raid on the Saturday afternoon—all got home safely but on Monday 19th Edith and David left for Starbeck once more, flying bombs (Doodle bugs!) had begun. There were two boys and a girl at Sunday school on July 2nd: C. E. met in the local Air Raid shelter. At a Deacons Meeting in Queens Road a bomb fell nearby and I have a mental picture of the Treasurer who wore a 'frock coat' on Sundays with his head under the table. Even in such circumstances one could see the funny side. Once more the hall was damaged.

July 19th the Methodist Church was damaged while I was there and once more the church was 'homeless' and met in the Mission Hall.

O. P. W. C. appears standing for Old People's Welfare Committee, after a Town Meeting at which I had made a comment leading to my membership.

The Superintendent of the parent Church Sunday School and I had planned a Sunday School camp at Blisworth, Northants. A good team of adult helpers had volunteered but with the advent of the Pilotless Planes as they were first called, the children had gone again, however a few remained and we went ahead with almost as many adults as children. Edith had agreed to do the cooking, leaving David with Grandma Starbeck. What courage and dedication she showed. I went ahead July 27th, having collected gifts of 'bread coupons', tinned meat, etc. and sent them by rail.

When I got to the church we were to use, I found there was no cooking arrangement, just an open fireplace. Scout camp style cooking was to be our task for the week. A local farmer let us have straw for palliasses which turned out to be barley and the horns got everywhere. The fire on which Edith cooked was made up of some old iron seat brackets and we used firewood the children collected and coal. How she coped I don't know. However we had a great team including Joan Wales and Nina Cole, candidates for the China Inland Mission. Young folk were led to Christ. One amusing thing was that Mr D. S. Jennings the Superintendent of Rye Lane, a bachelor of Victorian style but a great soul, went in his Sunday black suit and the railway lost his luggage so he wore it for the week. We had had so many food gifts that when I came to cash up I found that food per member worked out at just over 9/- each! So we began Sunday School Camps and Edith cooked for the next 22 as well.

On our return another strange thing happened in South London Tabernacle which had given the church a home and where Grandad Starbeck had been baptised. Mr Bamber was away and I was due to go on holiday on the Saturday but raids were on and the speaker planned cried off. I was asked to preach on the Sunday (the only time during Mr Bamber's 23 years as my minister—Only top preachers came to Rye Lane). So I took both services, rain came on the rostrum as I preached and heads went down as a warning sounded, however we had the communion service and I got the 11.13 p.m. train from Kings Cross to Harrogate due in at 8.11 a.m. I took two services at Starbeck Mission on Sept. 3rd and was home the following Tuesday—precious days.

Ted West came to the Mission at this time through one of our girls in his office. He has just returned from 41 years in India (1994).

Edith's mother died Sept. 27th. suddenly—how good Edith and David had so much time with her. I again travelled all night. The following Sunday I preached at Starbeck Mission on 'Jesus Wept' and 'This is life.'

Nov. 9th note says 'No Blackout'. At the Fireside Fellowship testimonies from Ron Barefoot, Sylvia Lewis and June Worboys, the latter married one of our boys and has been in touch this Christmas (1994), now a widow.

The Church took over an unused church in Benhill Road. Once more it had to be cleaned, lights and organ put in order, much hard work.

81 Flying bombs fell on our Borough, 190 people were killed, 1182 houses were destroyed and during the whole war 2254 houses were rendered useless.

I note that little David expressed his belief as follows: 'I thought that the life of you went to heaven when you die.' His Starbeck Grandad had instructed him about death.

During the bombing it was a habit to try and find out which church member had been bombed and to seek to help if possible. When George Drywood was with me he would cycle round to find out and I had many contacts of that kind. One occasion stands out. Two elderly lady members lived in a big house that had suffered badly and as they sat among the wreckage I tried to persuade them to leave their home and go to friends. They were reluctant to do so but I said the house was unsafe. As I stood and talked to them I leaned on the big marble mantle shelf over the fireplace and my elbow dislodged the lot and it fell in the hearth. They agreed to leave! One dear man told a very kind story years later. He said when his fiancée's home was bombed and her father was killed they had a lot of sympathy but that I went with a spade. One of the nicest things I heard, but it was all of grace.

1945

Feb. 27th: Oh Glad Day, 'Edith and David returned' to Muschamp Road. I note that in March Margaret Masters made confession of faith; of recent years Margaret has sent me a gift at Christmas and again this year (1994): Kept by the power of God.

At the end of the month it was said that the rocket attack was ended. These had been the most frightening of all the weapons for we heard the big bang and then the sound of them coming afterwards. I think I found them the worst. The Woolworth store in New Cross was wiped out in one attack.

April began with 'Up to bed for first time since last June'; evidently we had been sleeping downstairs. From July '44, I had been required to do A.F.S. (1 in 3 nights).

I wrote in Rye Lane Magazine a scheme 'from Cradle Roll to Church Roll'—good in theory but not in practice.

May 5th. notes 'Removal'. That would be when the owner of Muschamp house wished to return and we were offered use of 100 Pepys Road. David went to Waller Road School.

In June I had an X-ray for chest pain. In July we had our first Broadstairs Camp for North Peckham Children, Rye Lane Chapel first week. Edith cooked for 50 children and 9 adults. We ran a Scout Camp in August with just 12 boys.

At the end of the year I paid a tribute to the faithful band of workers in my report to H.Q. as follows:

'One cannot speak too highly of the workers who had made Mission work possible during these years, many of them shared the experience of being bombed during a meeting for Young People, took the bombing in their stride and continued their service in spite of flying bombs and rockets. Their heroic stand for Christian truth in the face of the enemy will soon be forgotten by many but to some of us it will live until we die.'

The drift back of children resulted in the year ending with 300 on Sunday School registers, of whom 45 were over 12 years of age—24 Cubs, 24 Scouts, 70 in G. L. B. and 100 members of the Women's Own.

Chapter 12
After the War

After the war Peckham was a very crowded area. The children came and went, but came most readily when it was time for the annual outing or Christmas. One year in particular I remember we took 200 names off the Sunday School roll but added a further 300. In our peak year we listed 590 children and young people after careful revision.

For 23 years Edith did the cooking for what we called the Sunday School camp. One year we took teenagers—splendid teenagers—and many of them came to Christ, some of whom I am still in touch with. I hear from them from Canada, South America, California, and South Africa and one recently came back from New Zealand and called in to see me. We really did teach them and taught them to pray. We had what we called a chain prayer when each one said just a sentence and so they learnt to pray. One of them has told me that I was always emphasising that they should have 'the mind of Christ'. I don't particularly remember this, but this lady assured me that it was so. They teased me that I also always referred to the letter to the Ephesians and I must admit that the old Bible I used is very heavily thumbed in that book perhaps because it is such a wonderful exposition of our unity in Christ.

The social implications of the gospel were not neglected either; we shared the founding of a Christian Old Peoples Home and I chaired the Camberwell Old People's Welfare Committee for many years. And in our home, to our great joy, our son had decided to be baptised when he was twelve, gained an assisted place in Dulwich College, took his BSc degree and subsequently entered Spurgeon's College and was ordained.

When we went to the North Peckham district we found a very poor but close-knit community, often living two families to a vermin infested house. Some doors were never locked; a shoe lace through a hole in the door gave access but as I visited door to door I always knocked, once for the folk downstairs and twice for the folk above! The Mission Centre had a good name as it had provided soup years before in near famine conditions and these things are not forgotten. I was known as the 'mission parson' but early on the young people gave me a useful nickname for they knew I hated the distant 'sir'. Over the years I was 'Boss' to hundreds and some, now grandparents, still use it.

The war had changed everything. 26 major incidents within half a mile of the Centre had left great gaps in every street. Now the area was being cleared for new estates and the old communities were dispersed. The Mission Hall had not escaped. Bomb damage repairs revealed that a main beam resting on two pillars supporting the upper floor was unsafe. We had to close the upper Hall and hired a day school but the work was greatly hindered. The builder held out little hope of replacement as supplies were short. Of course we prayed. One day soon after the builder came to say that 'a strange thing had happened last evening'. He had been reading the Evening News and saw an advert for a R. S. J. and it was just the right size and length for the chapel. Now was that a coincidence?

Edith was a great home-maker. We were never bombed out, but due partly to the war and for economic reasons, we lived in six dwellings during our Peckham ministry, until the church provided us with a house in chapel grounds, where we lived for twenty happy years. A great variety of people were entertained—visiting preachers well known in evangelical circles, young folk needing a hide-out when things got too difficult at home. I said that men from the local "spike" had a mark on our gate.

We had begun our ministry with the words of Washington Gladdens hymn in mind:

O Master, let me walk with Thee
In lowly paths of service free:
Thy secret tell, help me to bear
The strain of toil, the fret of care.

Help me the slow of heart to move
By some clear winning word of love.
Teach me the wayward feet to stay
And guide them in the homeward way

It was our joy to present the good news to the young and old of Peckham for many years—the 'joyful news of sins forgiven' because the Lord Jesus had died for our sins at Calvary and was risen to be a living Saviour.

1946 began with a comparison with the start of 1945 as follows: Seniors 16 became Christian Youth Group 43. Juniors 58 changed to 170, Primary 44 to 110 and North Peckham Baptist Mission appears instead of the old name of James Grove Hall, as the previous name of the road had changed to East Surrey Grove years before!

Edith's father died on Feb. 26th, and Edith went at once. David and I followed to Pilmoor on the 28th. returning March 4th.

I note that David now had bantam chicks.

Camp had been planned for Bexhill and that went ahead with Edith doing the cooking but I was in hospital for a month. After tests it was concluded that I had was suffering from the strain of the war years and no further treatment was given. Mr Metheringham took charge of camp and China Inland Mission missionary Mr Keeble took devotional periods I believe. It went well. Mother and Dad visited us that summer.

14 Young people associated with the Mission joined the Church. The fact that the parent church was out of its home put added responsibilities on the Mission but it gave big opportunities for service.

My report to L.C.M. says 'we had 665 children and Young People on the register at the year end. It is quite normal to have 300 present on Sunday afternoon. 50 Teachers! Every Sunday sees a small number waiting to join and we do not recruit as we have difficulty in coping. ' I note we were seeking a building licence for a hut so that we could start Beginners Department again. Christian Youth Group with 50 members filled the small back room of the hall, with Primary next door and Intermediate School filling the upper hall. All singing at once! There was a steady 'trickle' of professions of faith at this time as there had been over the years. We had pastors from Norway on two occasions who complimented us on Y. P. work.

1947

I note that David went to Music Lessons in January, was this the start? Edith was under strain which was not surprising and a short holiday was arranged. I think the L.C.M. helped with a visit to Felixstowe.

Apart from Deputation for the L.C.M. I had opportunity to address Nurses Christian Unions and other C.U. meetings but was under strain and on the sick list in March. Preaching most Sunday evenings it was a joy to have so many Young People there. We had a licence for rations for the Club and I note Bread Units and allowance for milk and tea.

June 17th. was 'high day' when the Nissen Hut was delivered but it looked like a load of scrap iron. We had spent all the £100 allowed by building licence on the required deep foundation so all else had to be voluntary. There was a metal frame, wooden long beams and lots of rusty curved sheet metal strips. Each one had to be wire brushed and painted. The architect said we could not have a door in the side of a Nissen hut but we devised one and a few non-churchgoing parents came to help the splendid team of helpers. My L.C.M. report says that a policeman was converted as a result but I cannot remember that. However it was duly erected and transformed youth work in that we had a useful meeting place for the Christian Youth Group on Sunday afternoon—soon it too was full. I had a wonderful elderly helper named Mr Ward, retired but with a young heart. Edith played for us and we shared leadership. Occasionally I would go outside and hear four lots of singing going on. The hut was in use for 16 years and at the end I noted that 500 young people had attended there. I still pray for them.

Open air meetings were held on Sunday evenings whenever possible and I note that nearly all the regular supporters were under 24 years of age and they chose to keep going through the winter. There was a Scout Camp and 40 came to the Sunday School Camp. We had a holiday in July: Kings Cross 1.0. p.m., Pilmoor 6. 5. A Youth Club Dinner before Christmas saw 44 Young People there and 10 adults, including our beloved pastor T. M. Bamber. The returning members who had been in the forces were very ready to come and work with the Mission.

1948

A strange experience of possible Divine healing took place. I was asked to visit a lady not expected to live. Going to the hospital I was given a gown etc. to wear to go into the ward for prayer. Later when she recovered she told me that she recalled my hand reaching out to her and drawing her back to life.

We began the year with 27 Beginners, 207 Primary, 273 Juniors and 63 in the Christian Youth Group. It is interesting to note that on revising the registers we found that 200 children had dropped out and 300 had joined. Coming from non-christian homes they just pleased themselves. Total after revision: 570.

A holiday in Yorkshire and then Scout Camp early in August. At some time we had been forced to move upstairs at 100 Pepys Road as the son of the owner returned from war service. When one of us lost hold of the front door in a high wind and the new owner complained, it drove Edith and me to our knees together in prayer. Mr Ramsey, the Church Secretary, secured the use of the church owned house at the back of the chapel for our use and we began the year in what proved to be a happy home for many years, 2 Cerise Road.

No 2 Cerise Road was one of three houses owned by the chapel: one was destroyed when the chapel was bombed and the others were damaged. Prisoners of war were used to restore them, turning the outside toilet to open from the kitchen and using dark brown paint everywhere. They were then requisitioned by the government. Mr Ramsey found that each church was entitled to one house for ministry. Mr Bamber had his own house, so a fight for chapel use was taken to the Minister of State and we were installed subject to subletting two rooms. Living on chapel property involved Edith and me in a new way with the parent church, leading eventually to Edith leading the catering committee, responsible on occasion for 300 at tea and to her doing the flowers etc. etc.

1949

We began the year with a small increase in the Sunday School and Youth Group. After revision we had 39 girls and 29 boys in the Group, and the total children and young people was 591. There were 53 in the Youth Club.

For Rye Lane Chapel to be reopened, basic repairs to roof etc. were permitted but decorations etc. had to be done on a voluntary basis—all hands to the task. I found myself doing the buying of materials etc. on behalf of the chapel and sharing the work with many. Being 'on the job' and within walking distance of the Mission was a great help to us all. David went by tram to Waller Road School and was christened Pythagoras by his teacher—religious and good at maths.

1950

Mission work went on as usual and I reported to the L.C.M. that 445 children and young people were present on one Sunday afternoon. About 40 went to camp including a number of teenage members. There is an interesting record of Young People's activities in addition to the adult services and prayer meetings as follows: Cradle Roll, Beginners, Junior school, Christian Youth Group Sunday, Monday Cub Pack "A" (20/24), Girls Club 30/40, Young People's Society of Christian Endeavour and Senior C. E. , Tuesday Sunshine Hour for Children—up to 100, Boys Club 30-40 in a school. Wednesday Girls Brigade all ages up to 90, Thursday Junior C. E. , Junior Bible Study (small), Senior Bible Study (late teens 6/10), Friday Cub Pack "B" 20-40, followed by Scouts 12/20, Saturday Youth Club 30/40. On Saturday afternoon there was Netball for Girls and Cricket or Football for boys according to season.

I note that the Baptist Revival Fellowship led by Mr Bamber had an All Night of Prayer in April. I remember it well. It seems I was on the London Baptist Association Committee at some time. Involvement with the Old People's Welfare took some time. I was able to address quite a few Christian Unions—Board of Trade etc. midday—and had some deputation meetings to take for L.C.M. It seemed I preached in Hull 'with a view'. Why I was unsettled is not clear but new rules came out for L.C.M 's after the war that disturbed me. How thankful I am that I was not invited to go again.

I recall cycling past Dulwich College and feeling resentment that my boy could never go there. I have often said that God heard me and said he would show me. We had some help from Mr Frank Bussey in the clothing trade with trousers and from parents of older scholars with their used items and we got by.

1951

The year began again with high numbers in the Sunday School—567 after the usual revision of the roll. Only four Sunday Schools in the London Baptist Association had more scholars than North Peckham.

A new departure was the beginning of Holiday Club periods. Many children who would not attend Sunday School came at half term or Summer holiday periods, strange to say regular scholars did not find them so attractive.

I note that I joined a class at London Bible College in an attempt to learn Greek but was disappointed to find that my English was too poor to cope and I had to withdraw. I have never recovered from poor schooling but God has graciously seen fit to make some use of me and perhaps if I had been better trained I might have been less useful to poor people.

Another new departure which again shows wonderful grace on the part of Edith and her helper Vera Iveson: We ran two weeks at 'Camp' as we called the holiday in a school. One week for Juniors and one week for teenagers. We had a holiday in April at Pilmoor & Harrogate.

I note that we were to return our Ration Books in July—was this the end of food rationing I wonder?

Mrs Whincop, leader of the Women's Own arranged for us to have a week long holiday in Eastbourne; she was a dear friend. I think this was the time also when we looked after the Mission house for Mr & Mrs Bamber while they were away. I did church visiting and much else when the Pastor was away.

We entertained a good deal and Capt. J. C. Metcalfe often stayed with us when we shared meetings of the Overcomer Trust. I believe Joan Wales would leave for service in China at this time. She had worked with me in training for a time and we are still in touch (1995).

We had a Watch-Night service Dec. 31st as was usual in those days. During this year I had discovered that the Government were prepared to help finance Old People's homes by local loans, this through work with Camberwell O. P. Welfare which was taking up quite a bit of time. As a result I was working with Mr D. S. Jennings and solicitor Mr Lyon, looking for a suitable property for what was to become South East London Baptist Homes.

1952

A visit to Great Holland near Clackton early in the year prepared the way for Camp later on. That two week camp proved to be one of the best. The Church had given me a new B. S. A. Motor Cycle and I went on that.

Opportunities were given to address Youth Rallies in the Horsham area. A coach called at various villages towards a central point. There was real blessing.

In February I note I was to meet Mr Jennings at 147 Barry Road, the first mention of the house we were to buy for the Old People's Home and there is the first reference to S. E. London Homes Ltd. I visited the Overcomer Conference and evidently was already a Trustee. The rest of the work went on as usual. I believe Mr and Mrs Bamber were in the U. S. A. for a time. If so Edith would do the flowers in church—quite a job, but she enjoyed it. I believe David was baptised this year. He was a constant joy to us.

1953

I noted that we had children from 400 homes and that of 40 Young People in the Youth Group only one came from a home where parents would be in regular attendance at a place of worship. There were still over 500 in the Sunday School and 100 in the Women's Meeting.

We opened the Old People's home at THE ELMS, 147 Barry Road on June 6th. Several Old People had been in residence for some time. I note £8.0.0 so I think that would be our salary per week.

We started to have a Day of Prayer at the Hall, starting at 8.0 a.m. and using the available hours for prayer between services etc. Mostly men were free to come. Mr Bamber still had the occasional night of prayer. There is a significant note in my annual report which indicates how, within the limits of her physical strength, Edith shared the ministry with me. "Some of the girls come from homes where there is real opposition and almost persecution, their stories of trouble at home as told to my wife and me would make interesting reading but they are locked away. At times we feel like the parents of a large family and wonder who will be in difficulty next."

Two weeks camp was at Gt. Holland again with blessing. We still saw a steady trickle of confessions of faith.

1954

The visit of Dr. Billy Graham to Harringay now took a good deal of time as I was asked to arrange coaches. The first night we took a full coach and only three or four got in. The crowd, though orderly, was frightening until mounted police arrived. We had to wait for the 'few'—ticketing had gone wrong.

We arranged for about 1500 visits to Harringay and—a major effort—500 to the final Rally at Wembley. I was asked to do 'follow up' and was very disappointed. Those previously 'prepared' knew what they were doing when they 'went forward', but many did not have a clue.

We had over 60 in Christian Youth Group and when we took a party to Southend and the Coach driver saw the lads, he said he thought he had a load of 'Teddy Boys' and 'did they drink?' He need not have worried they were there on time when we set off back. From October to Christmas I noted there were only four evenings when there was no commitment of some sort. We had 'teams' from Kings College Hospital etc. for some evening services.

Hospital visiting was in the picture and I report that 40 were visited, some through an almoner. At some time Edith went with me to the one dealing with old people once a week.

The O. P. Welfare set out to found a club for shut-in folk, said to be the first in the country—we were pioneers in the field and I gave some time to it.

Again we had two weeks camp—2 parties, perhaps on the Isle of Wight.

I would take David to Harrogate on the motor cycle, Edith went by train for the fortnight.

1955

We had an average of 41 at the Christian Youth Group this year, but we were beginning to see them 'gang up' though many attended the Evening service in the Hall. As secretary to the Billy Graham Relay Committee I had happy fellowship with local ministers and clergy and we did see some real blessing. Camp on the Isle of Wight was 'mixed'. The first week with 20 children and 10 young people was fine but the second week with older lads and girls not so good. One amusing episode: I was out in Ryde High Street paying bills when amid the crowds of shoppers a group of older girls ganged up on me and stood across the road shouting "Dad, Dad". I wonder what the shoppers thought of such a father!

Sunday School was smaller now but still over 400—it had reached its peak. About 70 was usual on Sunday evenings when I usually preached.

1956

I ought to make it clear that I did not keep a diary, just an engagement book, but my annual report to the L.C.M shows what satisfaction I found in presenting the gospel to people in hospital etc. There is quite a list of, mostly, elderly folk.

It is good to read that the camp on the Isle of Wight was a time of blessing, both weeks went well and it would seem that the previous group problem had passed. I believe I had a van by this time, a Ford 5 cwt that was pre-war and had been used by the O. P. Welfare for meals-on-wheels. I paid £55 for it! To get off the Island one had to queue and I had been told to come early in the morning to get a place instead of my late booking. In the event I queued all day and had to race back to the ferry to be there to see the party across. Holiday was at Pilmoor and I note I came back by York, either by van or motor cycle. David used to spend his holiday at Pilmoor and district.

I note that Bob Hilbourne B. Sc had become a church member after his confession of Christ one Sunday evening in the hall and that he was teaching. Terry Muir would be teaching too—later they were to marry.

"I" must appear again and again in this record but it was all of grace that we were sustained. Edith had a breakdown about this time and needed much care but still managed to do the cooking for Camp—again a triumph of grace.

1957

Many changes were taking place at this time. David was accepted for Leeds University and went there in the Autumn, a big change for Edith and me as well as for him.

The Youth Club was losing its appeal—Rock and Roll got hold of the Young People—but we still had about 50 at Christian Youth Group.

The advent of West Indians began to make a difference in the district, one fine old lady, restored by grace, made a fine testimony. She greeted me, when asked how she was, "Oh rejoicing in the Lord brother."

The Mission sent me to Marlow Bottom for the Sunday School anniversary and as Norman Quick moved to Marlow we visited them. He gave financial support while David was away for many years. Camp was again at Herne Bay two weeks and saw some blessing. I could report on some confessions of faith as God had given us year by year. I think we all had a holiday at Felixstowe as the Mission allowed David to go. All the usual work went on day by day.

1958

I note that the King George 6th Club was opened for disabled people and a Princess opened it. I had served on the Committee. We had the Easter weekend with Mr & Mrs Quick at Marlow and I would preach. I think we had another car and had a holiday in Yorkshire, went to Ingleton, Bedale etc. as well as Harrogate and Pilmoor.

I believe there was some danger of the Mission Hall being cleared with the rest of the district. Mr Ramsey (Church Secretary) and I went to County Hall, they said it was in Camberwell area—later I went to Camberwell Town Hall and they did not recognise it as on their area. So God preserved it.

From time to time there was evidence of the wonderful grace of God over many years; an elderly contact revealed that a former city missionary had presented the gospel at work years before and then in old age they came to Christ. One personal instance is reported to L.C.M I had gone to Camberwell Green seeking plants for Christmas gifts when a lady stopped me and said, "I think I know you". She was Mrs Sharp whose husband I had seen saved 15 years before. She and her daughter had apparently been unmoved. Now she told me she had been converted through an Elim Church.

Christian Youth Group had been reduced to about two dozen, where once it had been 60+. Rock & Roll had hit them but we had a very good Camp at Herne Bay—a crowd of children the first week and 20 Young People the second and much blessing.

1959

We had a Campaign in the hall and there was some blessing but the leader was being followed about by a woman admirer who came each evening. How clever Satan can be. The two men stayed in our home spending hours on recordings. Edith coped with them as with so much hospitality. We usually had visiting Rye Lane ministers to stay.

We had help from 4 City Missionaries preparing for the Campaign and visited over 2,000 homes. We had the Salvation Army Band for a March of Witness, 80 Young People from G. L. B. Scouts etc. adults. The average of congregations over 15 nights was 117 and we had 60 at the Prayer Meeting at the end. A children's effort alongside saw 100 children each day. Some people joined the church as a result, but blessing was limited I fear.

Again we spent Easter at Marlow with the Quick family.

Major building work started at Rye Lane and I was much involved with some measure of oversight.

We went to Pilmoor by car in June—Harrogate, Leeds etc. I preached at Henfield, Sussex and admired the area. Later I was invited to be Pastor thinking I was of retirement age! Edith and I loved the area. Years later we said God got us as near as possible at Speldhurst.

I had a Missionary Trainee with me, a fine young man but he did not stay in the L.C.M very long. We visited a great deal in new flats and one day we heard children screaming in a flat. Looking through the letter box I saw water coming down the stairs. We could not get in but as we waited the mother came up from the basement and let us in to help clear up the mess. No sink overflow.

Many people arrived from the West Indies but we found it difficult to get them in. I had a black evangelist to preach but only four black people came in.

Through a request from Maudsley Hospital I was able to visit a patient for them, seeking to bring peace to a needy soul.

Scout Camp was at Walmer; little did I know that later I would be involved with the care of the holiday home there.

1960

All the usual meetings went on and there were increasing calls by L.C.M for deputation addresses, midweek or Sunday, but I was not asked to go for longer periods as many men did.

We had our holiday in June and were at Leeds to see David get his B.Sc. presented by the Princess Royal. We travelled 600 miles which seemed a long way in those days.

One of our Sunday School Teachers was taken ill in Dawlish and I went to bring back his car and members of the family. The L.C.M were always most helpful in setting me free to help.

It would appear that we reverted to one week at camp. On the Sunday after camp I used the illustration that "a tramp is never lost because he isn't going anywhere". This led to the conversion of the brother of one of our Young People who later married one of our fine young girls.

On one Sunday we had 18 boys and 16 girls in the Christian Youth Group. About 45 people co-operated with the 'Days of Prayer' Sundays three times a year when we had about 6 hours together.

Gertrude Chambers, sister of Oswald whom I had visited regularly, died during the year. Recently I co-operated with the author of a book on Oswald Chamber's life (1994).

We had a fortnight holiday at Walmer. I had another trainee missionary with me this year. I paid one of my frequent deputation visits to Sevenoaks and to the Secretary Miss Raper. Little did I know that I would live to attend the prayer meeting with Edith when living near by. David went to Spurgeon's College in the Autumn.

Edith took over leadership of the 50 strong Women's Meeting during the year. When we went to Peckham in 1938 we found a very fine Women's Meeting led by Mrs Whincop. She had at one time been quite well off—a real lady—but after her husband died was ill advised and lost much, but still had a big house in Herne Hill, where she lived with her friend Miss Burgess. They were good to us, loaned us their little car, and during the war often gave me a meal.

The women's meeting had an average attendance of about 85 when we went. Mrs Whincop did a lot of visiting and I helped. When she gave up in 1960 Edith, who had helped in that work, took over the leadership. The attached note reveals something of the quality of my dear one.

She wrote: Feel most inadequate to follow the one we all loved so much, and from whom we all learned so much over these years. I shall not try to be Mrs Whincop, that I could never be, but I do want to be the friend of each one of you, and I hope you will feel you can talk to me just whenever you want to—I shall pray for each one of you, and I hope you will pray for me, and that this meeting will go on from strength to strength; but most of all, that many of you will even yet be led to know the Saviour.

The average attendance at that time was about 50.

1961

The slow decline in the numbers attending Sunday School and Youth Group went on, and the year began with 291 after the usual revision.

Once again I was responsible for the Billy Graham relays and while we saw reduced numbers there were some remarkable conversions. One man with M. S. brought by a business man who had himself been converted at Harringay, asked a steward to help him to rise and indicate his response to the appeal. He made a remarkable witness in hospital.

We had a holiday in Yorkshire by car and to many interesting places. I seem to have taken many more 'outside' meeting for the L.C.M , S. S. Anniversary Services etc. during the year.

Mr Bamber had moved away and Edith provided for him at weekends for quite some time. A special joy to us both.

My report to H.Q. indicates that I had become Chairman of the O. P. Welfare in Camberwell. This came about in a peculiar way. Canon Bishop the Vicar of Camberwell was to retire and had been chairman. He asked if I would stand for election but I said the City Mission would not permit this. Some time later I had a phone call from the General Secretary of the Mission suggesting I should take it. The Borough Council financed C. O. P. W. A. so there was no fund raising. £13,000 came that way. New responsibilities came this way and with the arrival of the new minister at Rye Lane Chapel, Rev. Emrys Davies.

A new venture was a special class for lads of the football team at 4.0 p.m. after Sunday School and Christian Youth Group and this went on for some time. Then someone started Sunday football for them and we lost them. Now the G. L. B. had a band.

1962

This was an interesting year for work and blessing among older folk, as well as the continued ministry among a reduced number of children and young people. The district was being cleared ready for re-building. Edith saw blessing with about 60 members present at the Women's Meeting she led. I believe we had a minibus and I collected members from outside the immediate area. I note that a Mr Irons died early in the year. He had been a member of a Baptist church, started a shop, opened it on Sunday and became a backslider. We were 'registered' with him when in Cator Street and he took a delight in seeking to embarrass me before women in the shop. His wife was restored to membership and the children came to the Hall. When his shop escaped fire bombs, he was impressed but not repentant. I lived to see him seeking forgiveness and he later joined another Baptist Church. O wonderful grace of God! His daughter leads the Women's Meeting in North Peckham having been converted in my early days at North Peckham (1994).

I led a Men's Meeting at Rye Lane at this time, there was a business women's meeting at North Peckham and Mr Davies started a late night effort in the Chapel once a month which went on until 1.0 a.m. I found that a great strain as there was a full day to begin early next morning (Sunday). However we saw some very interesting people. I made another visit to Horsham Youth Rally where 2 confessed faith. Several of our own Young People were baptised in the year.

We had a holiday in June and I took services at Harrogate Town Mission and at Starbeck. We went to Ilkley, Ripon, etc. etc. When we got home we found that the house had been broken into and the whole place ransacked; it was weeks before we discovered what had gone. Edith took this in her stride in a wonderful way but we were shaken. Later we suspected a young contact we had befriended but we shall never know—certainly he did go to prison for theft later. There was the usual Camp for one week in August. Once more I was at Sevenoaks for the Missionary Exhibition.

It would be at this time that I became responsible for the Church Magazine. Often Mr Bamber would phone on Wednesday morning to say I had not written anything and to get a page in by lunch time. It came to our home on Friday. Now Mr Davies did not edit it and we had a Committee but I was left to put it to bed. This did mean a reduced amount of time given to door to door visiting but the L.C.M did not complain. Two Saturdays a month two of us shared an Open Air witness on the chapel steps. There is a photo taken by a reporter for a Christian Paper of this. It would seem that the Youth Club had given way to a Saturday Fellowship by this time; it would seem we were going for quality not quantity in the changed district circumstances. But how richly God blessed us—His grace is wonderful.

I did a review of the work and found that the average attendance at 6.30 on Sundays was 63; we were in touch with about

250 children and Y. P. and Edith often had 60 at the Women's Meeting.

1963

I noted this year that since 1948 we had contacted 2159 children and young people in the Hall and of these about 500 were teenagers; many of the latter showed signs of grace, but how many went on to know the Lord? Some did and I am in touch with a few in 1994.

The father of one of our girls, June Warboys, was very ill and my Doctor and his said 'this man cannot die—do you know a priest who can visit him?' They sent for me. I had never met him but knew he had been antagonistic. He listened and made confession of faith. The following day June phoned Edith to say he could not remember my visit and Edith said 'Why do you not talk to him?' Which she did. I visited again and found that he really had come to faith (March 19, 1963).

I took a lady to stay with friends at Chingford. Little did I know we would live there. We had a holiday in May, went to Pilmoor, Harrogate, to May at Crimple, preached at Starbeck, to Thirsk, Hambleton Hills, Leeds, Otley, Masham, Hinderwell. Cost of travel: £8.10.0. 991 miles.

About this time there was a crisis. A Finance Committee concluded work could not be done at North Peckham. I asked Edith if I should fight it or resign. I fought it and the Rebuilding Fund was kept open and work put in hand in due course to transform the rear of the Mission premises.

David and Maureen were married July 27th—more sewing done by Edith. Pa was with us and an interesting thing happened. I lost my only car key and needed the car for later in the day. Eventually Pa came to me with the key and I said 'how did you find them'—He said "Oh I asked Father to show me where they were." Such was his faith in God!

Camp was Aug. 17—24 and I note that we had a good camp. Average attendance at the evening service was said to be 76.

One remarkable contact came through a Meter Reader who reported to the Chapel Caretaker of a needy old lady. I visited but was rebuffed until I took her apples I had collected from near Sevenoaks. So began a 'fruitful' time of real help and fellowship. We had a late holiday at Walmer and I went fishing most days as Edith just enjoyed sitting reading. Once again I was at Sevenoaks for the L.C.M. I note that one Wednesday I collected the Magazine proofs at 2.30, pasted it up etc. and returned it to the printer at 11.0 p.m. It would be at 2 Cerise Road on the Friday for distribution on the Sunday. This was no small task for it was not a small magazine.

The district was being cleared for the North Peckham Development Area. A new feature had developed in Holiday Clubs for Children when for a week over 100 children would be brought together for games and a Christian message.

There was a sad experience during the year: one of our 'Mission girls' was to marry at Rye Lane and the bridegroom failed to turn up.

1964

Women's Own. This year we rejoiced to have 17 new members in spite of the area being cleared. We were contacting a new area beyond the old City Mission district and Edith had a fine meeting with members bringing Bible Texts on a subject each week etc. The Mission was always a friendly place but it was good to hear a girl from a new estate say, "Oh I love this place, it is like another home". Sunday School was down to 254 as we endeavoured to get children transferred to other Sunday Schools on removal. I note that I rarely had a free evening. After many years in which the local High Church was not friendly towards what one vicar described as 'some sort of conventicle', a new friendly vicar came and invited me to preach at their Harvest Thanksgiving service and he came to us on special occasions.

We spent a good deal of time seeking to help the wife of a heavy drinker; from time to time we had her in our home and we had the children to stay. She was very fond of Edith and made a confession of faith. She still sends me a Birthday card in 1994. There is quite a story here but it must remain untold apart from saying that I collected her in the middle of the night from a Police Station in South London on one occasion and from the home of a Vicar in North London late at night on another. She took an overdose in our home and tried to escape from the ambulance when she arrived at Hospital in my presence. Isn't God wonderful.

After many years of just friendly contact I was called by our next door neighbour—their sister had taken an overdose and was unconscious. I gave her the kiss of life and Edith called an ambulance. Later she was led to Christ and later still her husband too. She and her sister both left a little gift to us in their wills. I note that I had served on the O. P. Welfare Committee for 21 years and had been chairman latterly. The Story of the Elms is told elsewhere and of my chairmanship from the start.

We had a remarkable escape at this time when a man friend of one of the Mission young ladies found a home with us. He said he had been a Secret Service man and was well spoken. One evening when I had a study full of men teachers from the Sunday School I was called out and Mr Davies and the Church Secretary were there to reveal that he was a thief and challenged him. He threatened to kill me if I told the young lady. I said, "I shall go straight to heaven but you will have to face God". I gave him a day to tell the lady himself. We could so easily have handed him over to the police for I had a strong team of men but we let him go. Later he locked a hotel keeper in a room so that he could rifle the place; the hotel keeper escaped in his night clothes through the window. He found a milkman who helped him and the police were called to arrest this villain. He called on me some time later seeking the address of the girl but she had gone. I saw him out in my pyjamas and then found he had left a glove in the sitting room so he could come back again. I went out with it to his car in bare feet and got rid of him. We never saw him again.

David's ordination brought us much joy. Mr Bamber had dedicated, baptised, married him and Maureen and now shared the ordination. Having shared rooms upstairs in Cerise Road for a year, they left for Todmorden.

One of our very fine overseas Missionaries, Mary Taverner, was home from Peru and ill in Mildmay Mission Hospital. She asked for anointing and as I had done it before, fellow deacons asked me to preside as we gathered by her bed. She made it clear she was ready to accept the will of God and was seeking to obey Scripture. She died in peace some time later.

We had a short holiday in Spring. We went to Hutton-le-Hole with Hilda.

August 15th we were at Todmorden for David's Induction.

We had Christmas with David and Maureen and returned for the Holiday Club with up to 129 Children there.

It was at this time that I was asked to join the Committee of the Railway Mission. Eventually I got J. C. Metcalfe to join me and later I was Chairman for a period.

I had written in April about the slow progress of the Rebuilding Fund for work at the rear of the Mission. We had a special day of prayer about it. The General Account of the Mission was for £1584. 7.6. for 1963 compared with £191.10.0 in 1938 when I arrived.

We put on a Demonstration at Central Hall for the L.C.M Messenger Rally. Dennis Kemp arranged this and it went very well—we took over 100 to the meeting by coaches.

I noted for the readers of my Newsletter that David was beginning to see blessing at Todmorden and had his first Baptism. Also that "Baby Ruth" had arrived to add to their joy so we were Grandparents!

1965

The clearance of the area went on and we were informed that it would be 1968 before the building programme was complete. Once a month a group of nine or more members visited from door to door in the flats around our old district and the membership of the Women's Own held up, as did attendance at the evening service.

Holiday clubs were arranged as in previous years.

In April I had an unusual experience at the monthly meeting of the L. C. M's when we began to sing the hymn 'Loved with everlasting love', with the refrain 'I am His and he is mine'. I was overwhelmed in a wonderful way and had to stop singing: in fact in a way I was surprised that all the other missionaries did continue to sing. Perhaps I was under pressure and did need such a blessing from the Lord. I shall not easily forget the experience.

There seemed to be no end to committees: Deacon's, S. E. London Baptist Homes, Mission Council and each section had a committee, Camberwell O. P. Welfare, Railway Mission, etc. No wonder my report to H.Q. said I was tired.

We got a Minibus for the Mission. It cost £130 and the Undertaker friend, Mr Uden had it in his garage.

In June we went to Staithes at the beginning of the holiday, called at Pilmoor and Harrogate and on to Todmorden, back to Pilmoor and then home. On my return I had to share duty at a big Conference Centre with another missionary. We had a 'stand' presenting the Gospel. I think I also did Jury Service that year.

Camp was at Herne Bay, our favourite place. The evenings were a time of real blessing as I shared with the young folk some aspect of Gospel truth by flannelgraph etc. This was followed by a holiday at Walmer.

We had Christmas in Todmorden and went to Pilmoor too.

The Mission main hall had a Spring clean for once since repairs in 1949. The high ceiling we had never tackled but a friend got scaffolding and about 70 folk had a share in a major wash down. The 22 ft high ceiling looked better for a wash. With Dennis Kemp's help new lighting was added.

1966

My Newsletter in March is full of thanksgiving for the response to the Rebuilding Fund appeal. We began in 1963 with £918 in the Fund after major work over many months at Rye Lane Chapel. Some thought that nothing more could be done. In January of this year there was £7014 in hand. Again with the help of Dennis Kemp a boiler was installed and central heating added. Two of us were working on pipes and the question arose who should crawl into the narrow space under the platform. Ron Escott, quite a wag, said "You go, because you don't have as long to go as I have." That was in case I got stuck.

Mr Drywood presented his report on the work. He was a splendid help and a true friend to us both. He reported blessing in the evening services: Average congregation 75 and I had preached on 37 occasions.

The clearance of houses round the Mission Hall led to having to visit over a wide area, for people still came back to the Women's Meetings etc. and we had to follow them up.

In my annual report I mention that I had been impressed by one visit to a new West Indian contact. I will copy my report. 'Perhaps the most humbling was in the home of coloured people. I was asked in on my first visit and there were children present, one boy of about 7 went close to his mother as we began to talk about spiritual things and I tried to find out about her background then the mother turned to him and said "No dear! That's not Jesus! She then said "he wanted to know if you were Jesus"—I talked to the little boy about my Lord; how wonderful he is, But I felt humbled to the dust. Oh to reflect His grace!'

It was a year of hard work and few converts. We were very tired and thankful for the offer from my District Secretary, Mr E. G. Andrews, of an extra week holiday at Stow on the Wold. I had a shooting brake and Edith spent most of the week just laid out in the back of the car—it was a life saver.

We had the usual camp at Herne Bay and two weeks Holiday Clubs for children (165). I note that at Christmas I visited or wrote to about 80 elderly or sick folk.

The new halls and toilets were opened at a special service on June 18th. It was a day of profound thanksgiving. This was stage 5 of the rebuilding fund of the parent church; a remarkable achievement. I believe the total cost was about £10,000.

1967

It seems we went to Starbeck to collect Hilda for holiday, to Pilmoor, Staithes and back, then to Todmorden. We returned via Wharfedale etc. and then home. I note that we had spent £10.0.0—quite a lot for that day.

We took part in another Billy Graham Crusade. I was on the 'sick list' for a week in July—a very unusual happening.

We had a holiday at Martello Place, Felixstowe in September and note a force 9 gale and lots of rain. I went to Bournemouth for the Overcomer A. G. M. and to Henfield in Sussex. In November we went to Pilmoor on the Tuesday, to Todmorden on the Wednesday and home to Peckham on the Wednesday! We were there again for Christmas.

My Mission report referred to 40 special contacts in which I had been involved, including acting as 'male nurse' for the sister of one of our ladies who had had a stroke until relatives and friends could be organised.

Sunday School was down to about 140 with the clearance of the area. Holiday Clubs and Camp as usual. I am surprised at my claim to have visited 70 in hospital.

Camberwell O. P. Welfare had to link up with Southwark and Bermondsey and we now had a staff of four full time and one part time. We had over £16,000 from the Council for holidays chiropody clubs etc. but I note that I did not feel I wanted to continue with this larger responsibility for oversight as chairman.

I had been a Deacon for 27 years and ended my report for the year as follows: "whatever the future holds it is our deep desire to serve the Lord effectively, to bring glory to his name and sinners to His feet, and for His sake to serve our day and generation." This proved to be my last Annual Report as a Missionary.

1968

In the Holiday Clubs at Christmas and Easter we still had well over 100 children, many brought from nearby estates by bus and car. I reported to the Church that we had been given a memorial gift of £325 and bought a Commer Minibus. The sad side of my work is indicated in that I attended three funerals in the first week of the year. We had a week holiday going to Pilmoor, Starbeck and Todmorden. Once again I was in Sevenoaks to preach at the Baptist Church. Camp for one week at Herne Bay was one of the best. A singing group came out of it. I took quite a few Sunday Deputation Services for my District Secretary, E. G. Andrews.

In my Newsletter sent out after a gap or two years I note that eight tall cranes were creeping towards the Hall. St. Luke's Church, Bradfield Club and the Baptist Mission were mentioned as the remaining buildings in the area. The Mission was by far the older as St. Luke's had been rebuilt after bombing. We had lost many valuable workers, one to Bible College, one to U. S. A. and many others had to seek accommodation in other parts of London. We still had 40 to 50 on Sunday evenings.

I will give extra space to cover details of events later in the year after the News Letter mentioned had been sent out in June, for it was time for new pastures.

We were due to leave for a holiday in September 1968 and it was more than a surprise to be asked to see the General Secretary of the London City Mission without delay. I went for the interview with some trepidation. What had I done—or not done! Much to my surprise I was invited to consider joining the executive of the Mission as what was then known as a District Secretary. (Now they are more imposingly called 'Directors'.) I was not to be transferred but I was to go and pray about it. Imagine having a fortnight on holiday to find out what the will of God could be for us! The outcome was that, somewhat reluctantly, we agreed to the move. The friendly Vicar of our North Peckham parish said I was becoming a Bishop! I never looked at the move like that and neither did my colleagues at Headquarters. At the heart of the Executive were two C of E clergymen and two Free Church laymen.

Though I did not keep a diary, I did scribble among the engagements some interesting comments, texts etc. On Thursday Sept. 5th. I paid my last visits before leaving for holiday; when I got in there was a phone call from Rev. Duncan Whyte, the General Secretary of the L.C.M He said, "I understand you are going on holiday and I wanted to see you." I said, "I can come in the morning before we go." I had no idea what it could be about, but I was very disturbed and note 'A sleepless night!'

I got to the office about 10.0 a.m. and had to wait, his Secretary showed me into his room and when he came in he told me that he would like me to become a District Secretary. (Both Mr Wrintmore & Mr Andrews were due to retire.) He said the D. S. was "a gruelling job". My immediate response was, "I am too old, I am 58!" He said, "Yes I know you are but you can give us 7 years but will have to retire at 65. We are all new and you have a long experience of the Mission. We shall not press you, or move you but if you agree, we promise to replace you with another Missionary." I went across the road to phone Edith and say, "It is the D. Sec."

Hilda was to stay near the Walmer Holiday home but of course we could tell no-one. I wrote at once to Mr Bamber and to J . C. Metcalfe, asking for their advice. Phil. 4 v 11 is scribbled in, "I have learned... to be content". Edith and I were of course much exercised after 30 years in North Peckham. Mrs Hurford, a missionary's wife, was catering and put on a recording in the evening. of Catherine Ferrier singing 'Oh rest in the Lord!' She said later she knew we were troubled. On the Saturday morning Brother T. read Ps 27 and evidently emphasised v11 'Teach me, and lead me', and v14, 'wait!' Evidently we went to Dover to sit on the cliff and watch the ships and it was a lovely day. On the Sunday morning my set reading was Ezek. 2. 8, 'Hear what I say unto thee, be thou not rebellious. ' Mr Hurford read Ps. 32 v 8 at morning prayers, 'I will instruct thee and teach thee in the way which thou shalt go, I will guide thee with mine eye." On going to the Baptist chapel there was a text in the entrance: "I will guide thee with my counsel." Monday was fine and I went fishing. Tuesday we went to Dover again. On Wednesday 11th. Edith and I had the assurance that I should accept and I wrote to Mr Whyte that day:

"Dear Sir,

Mrs Turner and I have given due consideration to your kind and gracious offer and after much prayer we have come to the conclusion that it is the will of God I should accept it. If you wish to see me before the appointment is confirmed I will gladly come up for the day.

Knowing just a little of the manifold duties of our District Secretaries, and admiring their devotion I face the prospect of becoming one with a good deal of trepidation. In fact at the moment I seem to alternate between awareness of my inadequacy and a sense of the Lord's rebuke that after He has called me so clearly to the work I can doubt His divine grace to see me through.

We are both impressed by the timing of this call which seems to seal the conviction which has slowly replaced our natural reluctance to leave a people and a work we have loved so much for 30 years. We know we shall have to pass through a little valley of tears as we leave North Peckham so I hope you will not think I am fussing when I express concern lest the people I have worked with should hear of the appointment casually. If it is to be made known soon I would be grateful if you could let me know so that I can at least inform the Pastor and secretaries.

We have a family gathering of Mission Hall friends on Sept 28th and you are to visit us on the 29th.

I pray that God will equip me for the task and give me grace to labour for His glory."

The day after I got a letter from Mr Bamber in which he said that had he still been at Rye Lane he would not have been happy, but quoted 'coming to the kingdom for such a time as this' and so encouraging acceptance. In the morning I wrote in Ps. 138 vv3&8, 'strength... and the Lord will perfect that which concerneth me', and on the Saturday there is the note, 'I rejoice to do Thy will O God. ' All these texts when I was not in the habit of being guided by a single text or taking my guidance in quite that way! On the 13th I had a letter saying the appointment was not confirmed.

On the 19th Mr & Mrs Andrews came and we had a long chat together but neither of us mentioned the secretaryship—did he know? On the 20th I had a letter confirming that it had to go to the full committee. We were home that day. Janet and Norman Briarley were married on the Saturday and I had an urgent call to replace a Secretary at Colchester for their Harvest Services on the Sunday. When I got home we had to wait up for a car load of harvest gifts for 70 people from Horsham. I did my final Magazine work on the 24th and J. C. was with us for the Railway Mission Committee.

Rev. Duncan Whyte was the preacher planned for the 29th (Anniversary). I asked which area I was likely to serve in, North or South and he said he thought it would be North. In October I wrote my last Newsletter telling folk of the move, having already told the Mission Council and the Deacons. I met the Committee of the L.C.M on the 30th. and then I was offered either a Mission house or the option of a loan. Mr Dunkley the Accountant advised me to take the loan and to look for a house at not more than £4,500.

I ought to have mentioned that on Saturday 28th we had the Anniversary gathering when friends of chapel and mission celebrated our 30th anniversary by giving us a projector and screen. I wrote of the occasion as a 'bitter/sweet' occasion as we knew we were leaving and they did not.

I received greetings from my father, typed by Dorothy, for our 30th. Anniversary. Note his comment confirming what my mother said about my being dedicated at birth. How wonderful that we both had such godly parents.

Gate House
Pilmoor
Helperby
York

14th September, 1963.

Dear Friends,

Christian Greetings from Pilmoor, to you all on this happy event and to your Leaders, or as the young would say 'the bosses."

Just fancy! 30 years, a big slice of Bread is it not. Pulling down or building up. A company of wreckers said, "We could wreck the Pyramids." But could they build them?

S. M. was given to God when he was born so Praise God for leading and Guiding, for those that lose their Life in doing the will of God in His Service find the True Bread.

In Deut. 11:11-12, 'The land I give to thee is a land of hills and valleys. ' In the valleys we find the mist too. One has said I will lift my eyes to the hills of God. As we climb we must get well up the steep, one step at a time, and looking back we find the view wonderful. I will lift my eyes to the hills, which cometh my help from the Lord.

My dear friends, What is wanted is more builders of and for God, so if we can't be a movie star—keep smiling; don't look glum, make someone happy by saying here—I come from one child to you all.

In Christian Love,
H. TURNER.

Chapter 13

At Head Quarters

I note that I started at H.Q. on Oct. 7, working with Mr Wrintmore, and became the District Secretary (North of the Thames) on Oct. 2lst.

A dear old friend Miss Flood, when told we had to look for a house said, "but all the houses belong to God!" We had difficulty in finding anything within the range given but on the way home one evening I got a copy of 'The Evening News' and in it was an advert for 103 Normanshire Drive. I told Edith that it would have gone but she insisted that I should phone. It had 'gone' but the vendor took my telephone number. Later he phoned to say it was on the market again. When we told Miss Flood we might have a house she said, "what number?" When told she said, "Bless the Lord oh my soul" (Ps. 103!)

We had an extra loan, put all we had in and agreed £5,575. On enquiry Mr Dunkley thought we would be 2/6 a week better off (plus any gain on the house—not mentioned).

For Edith it was a costly move, leaving a multitude of friends for a lonely life in North London, but she did not complain.

Here is the letter she wrote to the Women's Meeting:

2 Cerise Road,
Peckham
S. E. l5.
30th. Sept. 1968
Dear Friends,

You will no doubt be surprised to receive this letter

from me, especially as I saw you all this afternoon. I should like to have been able to talk to you and give you this news personally but that has not been possible. It is hard enough to write the letter, but to have told you would have been harder still because I am letting you know of our impending departure from North Peckham. Mr Turner has been appointed District Secretary of the L.C.M. He is to work in North London and will take Mr Wrintmore's place.

We first had news of this on the morning when we went on holiday (Sept. 6th.), Mr Turner was called to the office before we went—he was offered the post and it was made clear he could turn it down if he wished. We spent the first few days on holiday with minds in a turmoil, but seeking to know the mind and will of God. Gradually it was made clear that we must go—difficult as that is going to be. You will understand that we cannot lightly brush aside a call we believe to be from God.

To leave you all and the dear women is going to be one of the hardest things of my life, we have been such a closely knit team and I thank God for every one of you, but he who has called will also give the grace.

I know we shall have your prayers.

Yours in His service

Edith M Turner

She had a very lively Women's Meeting Committee and addressed this letter to the members when she got home from the Meeting. It reveals so very clearly how one we were in seeking the Lord's will and then seeking to obey it. It also shows that she had counted the cost. It proved to be a big cost, as I was away at the Office all day and after we moved house on Jan. 2nd. 1969 she was a complete stranger in Chingford South and told me she went shopping just to meet people and have someone to talk to.

I knew that she had attended the Presbyterian Sunday School in Harrogate and that her father went to morning service there when Chalmers Lyon was the minister and then supported the Town Mission in the evening. I do not know what happened when Edith was 12 but it was the beginning of a life-long devotion to her Lord. The partner was part of the Lord's leading, then to Starbeck Mission, then to London City Mission, then house after house during the war after our call to Peckham, the eight years of the leadership of the Women's Meeting after having supported Mrs Whincop in the work for many years. Note the assurance of the grace that was to be given, and it was.

I was to have the oversight of the day to day work of the Mission's work north of the Thames with about 60 men in the area. For me it involved a change to office work and how thankful I was for the service of a dedicated lady secretary who knew far more about the work than I did. Miss Jean Dyer had already served 21 years as Secretary to my predecessor Mr F H Wrintmore and was to continue long after I retired. She had to retire on reaching the age limit after a remarkable 45 years.

I had always known that we had a staff of remarkable Missionaries and knew something of their respective dedicated wives. But in seven years at H.Q. I was to learn a great deal more. Some worked as Industrial Chaplains, some among 'down and outs', some with churches, as I had done, and some had independent Mission Centres. Some were Men of God who had left better paid jobs to seek to represent Christ to the masses living and working in London. Some from overseas had come to give the message of life to visitors from many lands. It was a great privilege to pastor them. The most difficult thing was to recommend the removal of a family from one part of London to another as a need arose. Again, we saw many remarkable answers to prayer as new fields of service opened to the Mission.

Having been in South London for 32 years I knew it well but North London was a 'closed book' and I had to learn my way around. I was responsible for deputation work 35 miles out from Charing Cross north of the river.

We spent Christmas 1968 in Todmorden and visited Pilmoor.

1969

Jan. 2nd we moved to 103 Normanshire Drive, South Chingford. We had had the stair carpet up for weeks, for we did not know it would take so long for the legal matters to be covered!

I was into all kinds of meetings at once. One of the first was to the Hall in which Sir John Laing was interested, and after years of visits from Mr Wrintmore they were 'looking me over' and I heard one of the ladies say rather begrudgingly, "He's quite nice!" I later met Sir John, a dear Christian gentleman. Another Horsham Youth Rally in February.

An interesting thing happened 1st December. Edith and I went to the Mission Hall at Harold Hill—well out of London.

While there, missionary wife Mrs Hider took Edith on one side and said, "Don't let him move us." (It was a major part of my job to recommend the movement of men.) On Jan. 22nd I was at Harold Hill again for Mr Hider's farewell on his appointment as District Secretary South. He is in that post (1995).

1970

The outstanding event in the Spring was the death of our dear Pastor of the first 23 years in Peckham, Mr T. M. Bamber. He once said from the pulpit, "I don't fear death, but I fear dying." He was on his way to a preaching appointment long after retirement, he got to the station, phoned his wife, got into the train, was seen to be ill, was taken out at the next station and he had died. I went to Torquay with a dear friend, Norman Quick, to the funeral; he had been Pastor of Rye Lane Chapel for 35 years.

We had a holiday in Wales, in a cottage owned by the Chairman and had a very happy stay.

I was delighted to welcome a young man from Germany as a Missionary in my area. It was a new departure for the Mission and it was not easy to get changes made. There was a 'Victorian' hangover, however Peter Shaub is still in the Mission working among overseas visitors. Our previous Secretaries wore black jackets and pinstripe trousers! Mr Hider and I had many a little battle with the old ways and got an extra week holiday for staff. We had a new car and the Mission helped us to keep it up to date as we did a lot of travelling.

Life was very full indeed. Whenever possible Edith went with me to Sunday appointments, and if I was out for the day

I tried to get an invitation for her too. In that way she met many new friends, otherwise she had a lonely life. She befriended the nextdoor neighbour and got friendly with the wife of the Secretary of the local Congregational Church which we attended when free.

It seems we visited David and family in Swadlincote, before the move to Rosemary Road, Birmingham.

For some time the Executive had shared the concern of the main Committee about the need for new headquarters. The lease of Eccleston Street was running out. I had a big office there which gave us a view of the guard going to and fro near Victoria Station. Staff often came in to see the band going to the Palace etc. At that time the Mission had the biggest legacy ever: the story went that a wealthy lady, Miss Billings, did not know where to leave her money and a solicitor suggested the L.C.M She lived at a place called Christmas Pie!

The Magazine reveals that a bombed church, St. John's near Tower Bridge had been purchased. Mr Hider and I decided to go and see the ruin. It had been cleared down to the crypt roof. We found a man at work and he said he had found some bones, so we told him to stop work and report to his boss. The outcome was the discovery of a crypt full of lead-lined coffins which had to be boxed and sent to Woking for reburial at considerable cost.

I had been responsible for the arrangement of the Annual Meeting at Central Hall, Westminster and Edith enjoyed doing the flowers for this big occasion.

The tea was a sick joke for many years. A few thin sand-wiches etc. went like the wind before about 150 men and their wives. I got North Peckham friends under the leadership of Vera Iveson, Edith's camp helper, to put on a worthy tea.

1971

Early in the year Mr Ball asked me to meet a member of St. Helen's Church of England, who was willing to bring a team to help with the Hall in Covent Garden. Sandy Miller was a young barrister, so we met early. He and his team were a real blessing in work among young people. (Now in 1995 he is a prominent clergyman at Holy Trinity where a very big crowd gather.) His team started what we called West End Outreach. There were 16 of them.

Numbers were being reduced as there had been no intake during the war and older men retired. I had about 60+ in my area when I went. Men came and went and I often was awake in the early hours thinking and praying about placements.

It would seem that I addressed two or three meetings most weeks as well as coping with office work. In April I went to Bexhill on deputation and it would be then that a house was offered to the Mission—it became three flats, two for retired folk, one for holidays. I did quite considerable mileage within the London area and note the car service cost £6 on one occasion!! Edith and I went to the Chelsea Flower Show in May. We had a week holiday at the end of the month and it says— Swadlincote, Staithes, Pilmoor 820 miles.

Following a conference we began meeting our missionaries in three groups. In July we had a week at Stow on the Wold and enjoyed that area very much. Upper & Lower Slaughter, Snowshill, Bourton on the Water etc! Stratford on Avon and

Studley Castle! Later we went to Marlow to Norman Quick's family for a weekend.

In October it seems we were at David's welcome at the Birmingham Churches. In October I note seven meetings in one week. I was at an Evangelists' Conference in December with Mr Hider.

At the year end I had two new jobs added: Secretary of Disabled Missionaries & Widows Fund, and Missionaries' Holiday Fund. E. G. Davies had retired. On handing over he said, "There's nothing to it brother". Then Miss Dyer asked for an appeal letter—later she brought in 1200 copies for me to sign. Nothing to it! She took this extra work in her stride. It involved hundreds of 'thank you' letters too.

1972

Soon after going to H.Q. I was faced with the fact that our Hall in Walthamstow had dry rot. Peter Trainer was missionary and after his wife stepped through the floor, the hall was sold. Peter was upset for he had a good meeting and Edith used to play for the Women's Meeting. Peter took a local pastorate but as an expert photographer he gave some time at H.Q. and I used to pick him up on my way. Peter is now Editor of the Magazine and a Deputation Secretary (1995).

In February I went to Kensit College to speak about the Mission. I was asked if we took ladies, and as so often I said we allow each man to marry one. I often teased Mr Whyte about admitting women and he said 'over my dead body'! Eileen Devenish was there and I said we needed a lady Secretary for Mr Hider. Later she was again faced with this need and came to H.Q. That began for her an interesting sequence of events. More later.

There was an opportunity for ministry at the Birmingham City Mission staff conference, one weekend in May. Once again we visited Yorkshire, and had two weeks at the cottage in Wales set aside for use by Mr Bartlett, the Chairman. We had a long weekend with Jessie Lynn. I made up a map of London with details of 'men at work' and noted that there were 21 Boroughs in my area of London.

The Mission, founded in 1835, has a long history of providing holidays for missionary staff. How they need a break from the pressure of life in inner London and the need to share time with their families! A new surprise came when at the end of 1971 we were asked to take on the oversight of Mission Holiday Homes. Whilst this added to my responsibilities at Headquarters and certainly added to the work of my faithful and efficient secretary, it brought Edith back into a closer share with me in service as my work at Headquarters had usually meant that I was in the office at about 9 o'clock until about 5 o'clock and often engaged in the evenings. When we took over there was one large house capable of catering for about 20, one smaller house with six large bedrooms (bequeathed to the Mission incidentally) and two cottages. Over the years we were able to open up four new centres and Edith was in her element for she was a great home-maker. These self-catering units were very popular. One was a delightful bungalow under the shadow of Cader Idris in Wales which had also been bequeathed to the Mission, another in Scotland and two in England.

1973

As usual the year began with a week of prayer but on the Friday evening we went to Martello Place, Felixtowe to begin the additional work with Holiday Homes. When we joined the Mission there was a lovely house at Eastbourne. It had been given to the Mission and was taken over in the war. Martello Place and some gardens being purchased for about £5500, Mr Andrews and his wife had done a good job there. On occasion it could take over 20 people. There was a cottage at Overstrand, near Cromer, which had to be cleared of bedding for the winter and we went there on Jan. 6th. in thick fog. There was dry rot in the place and it was damp. We cleared the bedding and took it to Martello Place. While I continued with a full programme on Sundays I had to take fewer midweek deputation appointments from now on.

I note 'Morris Marina £1033.31'. Can that have been a new car? I think it was. The diary says "New Car"—a much needed tool for the new job. For some reason we went to St Leonards by rail—a new opening for a holiday unit.

In February we left Eccleston Street and moved our office to the old vicarage near the new H.Q. to be. I had a small bedroom near Tower Bridge Road and suffered much from traffic noise. Mr Barr had recently become the accountant, Edith went to take care of their first child and met Mrs Barr out of hospital with her second. The Lord Mayor laid the foundation stone of the new H.Q. in March. Once more to Henfield, Sussex to preach.

Early in March we had the annual meeting held in the Guildhall instead of the Mansion House. In addition there were the Main Committee, five meetings to address and on the Friday Edith and I went to Walmer. Here there was the six bedroom house and the cottage to oversee. Back on the Saturday ready for the Sunday appointment. The following week three or four meetings and off to St Leonards Friday and Saturday to begin getting this new unit ready. The first of four we opened in our day. Home for morning and evening services to take on the Sunday. Not every week was like that. We had a party at Easter for H.Q. staff in Martello Place. It was usual to welcome each fortnightly party into Martello Place and Westwood, Walmer, pay bills etc. We had to spend a lot of time at St Leonards, getting it ready with some help. Edith made it into a home, covering every detail down to the last teaspoon, ready for each family. We had a few days in Yorkshire in June. On July 9th. we left for our Swiss holiday provided by Doris Green who was a worker in North Peckham when we went there. She wanted to celebrate our Ruby Wedding and as her sister had left her a house she gave us the holiday of a lifetime.

Five days by Lake Lucerne, near Mt. Pilatus and 5 days at Wengen, arranged by Parkinson's Christian holiday firm. Another link in two chains—Eileen, and our own future holidays. Wonderful sights and rich fellowship—we both enjoyed it to the full. On one occasion we were pressed to take a chairlift—getting on as it passed we were told it 'never left the ground very far: but when we looked down tractors looked like toys. Edith was very brave to venture. Someone paid for us to go to the top of the Jung Frau. The train stopped for us to look out on the face of the Eiger and we saw the ice carving of cars etc. at the top and dogs in the snow. Also walked on a glacier, a wonderful day out.

Later in the year my Secretary Jean Dyer had an operation and Doris Green came into the office to work.

David and family came to us for Christmas dinner and to stay.

1974

At the beginning of the year we visited Stow on the Wold where the L.C.M. had the use of limited holiday accommodation. Arranged payment etc.

It seemed we popped up to Birmingham just overnight at some weekends. At Derby for the Railway Mission A.G.M. in March, as speaker. Later in the month we stayed with ex-Rye Lane members in Maidenhead as I addressed meetings in a C. of E. church. Easter would be at Felixstowe with H.Q. Staff. Later to Walmer with caterer helper Mrs Hurford making Retired holidays possible. To Yorkshire for bank holiday in May. July saw us in charge of a Parkinson's holiday group, visiting Churchill's Grave on the way to Llandrindod Wells, Wales. About 30 in party, Devotions in evening. Visited Aber, Hereford, Brecon, Ludlow and a factory producing woollen articles from 'sheep to wearer', a happy party for a week. In August we were again at Plymp in Wales—Mr Bartlett's cottage. We enjoyed that lovely coast and on the first Friday went to try and find the bungalow at Arthog. Nearly gave up when a railwayman directed us.

Mr Barr came to us the following Wednesday, Thursday we were taken into the bungalow that had been left to the Mission. Spent the day exploring, clearing papers etc. Found receipts for 10/- a regular gift to L.C.M then Mr Parker left the Bungalow to the Mission! We called on Miss Toms in

Gloucester, one time worker in Peckham, on our way home well aware of the new task awaiting us in Arthog.

Retired folk were taken to look after Martello while staff had holidays. We had a holiday at Walmer in October.

I had the opportunity to introduce Tuse Kappers, a Dutchman, as Missionary to seamen at Tilbury, persuading the Committee to accept him and his German wife without the usual probationary period.

I note that I had taken the August Bible Study evenings at Rye Lane again. We moved into our new offices etc. at the end of November. My office about the same size as at Eccleston St. but all new. Two nights in Yorkshire late December. I imagine we spent Christmas in Birmingham as it says Sunday return after Lunch. Mr Young went to Walmer during the year and still there 95! and still preaching!

1975

I noted that the car had done 31,000 so we did get about a bit (Jan).

Jan. 19th says 'Stechford'—did I preach? We had a retreat with German Sisters of Mary late January (Executive prayer time).

There was the opportunity to introduce a telephone ministry in the new H.Q. I had been trying for four years! 407 9909!

March 20 was a great day. Opening of the new H.Q. began with police dog searching and then the arrival of the Queen Mother. She came into my office, met Hr Hider and me and stayed to talk for quite while, as her escort fidgeted to get a move on! Edith said I did not wash the hand she shook for some days—it wasn't true!

Our dear friend of many years, George Drywood died and I took part in the funeral.

April 9th we left for Arthog and called in Birmingham on way home, at weekend. End of April to Martello place, on to Sunny Corner to get it going and home (Monday to Wednesday).

About that time I had our Pension details and went to Mr Whyte to remind him I would be 65 in June. He said, "we have been left a bungalow in Speldhurst, go and see it and if it gels, you can go there!" May 1st we visited and Edith said, "Tell Mr Whyte that it 'gels'!"

About this time I had two remarkable experiences of the Lord overruling but I don't know the dates. For some time I had been in touch with the Post Office Christian Association Secretary and had addressed their Annual Meeting on 'Being Crucified with Christ and Risen in Him etc.' (They published it in their magazine and years later it appeared in a magazine in U. S. A. , but that is beside the point.) They supported Mr Payne as Post Office Missionary in East London but wanted one in the West. They arranged for me to meet 'top brass' and I took Mr Cobb as a possible missionary. There were about eight representatives when one Postman's Union rep said, "I'm a Roman Catholic and you will never convert me." They laughed and he told how he had been a communist, called on a Priest, was not welcomed, went to another. He said I was not going to be put off by one disciple (ref. Judas). He then said, "I can't see any reason why this man should not visit us." That seemed to be the turning point and we were assured of a welcome for the missionary and the provision of a pass. He was warned not to go to one place as it was communistic. Mr Cobb was accepted, served for some time and was followed by another. We went to another area manager etc. the following day and again were accepted, so most of London was covered.

The second experience came about through the interest of a Mr Chilton whom I met on deputation to Watford. We had four men working with British Rail north of the river, but some years before ceased to have anyone in the south. An Industrial Mission Church of England may have been the cause. Mr C. knew of our desire and phoned me one day to say that if we acted quickly an area manager, shortly to retire, might be sympathetic. Mr Hider asked me to process this. The interview went fairly well and in the end we were offered a pass for travel and authority for Mr Chubb to visit staff over a very wide area south of the river. I believe two more have joined him (1995).

To Arthog again in May to get it ready. Later we were packed to visit Yorkshire when the car broke down at the bottom of Normanshire Drive (gearbox trouble). A friendly car repairer took our luggage home and I went seeking a car hire, found one out of London and we used that. The Marina gearbox gave a lot of trouble.

To Wales again with a holiday party in July. Was this the occasion when we met Archie Barton, a widower, Eileen Devenish (Mr Hider's Secretary) being shown our Swiss slides booked to go, met Archie and later asked me to 'give her away' on Marriage to him. 16 years 'good' followed.

In July Edith and I were invited to stay with the Mission Chairman, Mr Bartlett and his wife at Ledbury, Glos. A delightful weekend when I preached at their chapel and had the joy of seeing his chauffeur in the service. I had often chatted to him when be brought Mr Bartlett to committees.

August: Took Rye Lane Bible studies again and preached on Sunday. In August we had holiday at Arthog and note David and family joined us (Day Only ?) how we enjoyed these periods of relaxation at Arthog. Lots of fishing etc. I note "Allegro £1118 less £875 new car. I note the telephone ministry had 2443 calls in 7 months.

In September we were at Rye Lane for the Mission Anniversary and note "As I was with Moses, I will be with you". On October 9th I note that I was to preach at Divisional Day when all the Mission would be present—in effect my farewell.

November 19th we moved to Rodborough having sold 105 Normanshire Drive, repaid the loan and had a considerable sum (for us) in the bank ready for further use. There were several gifts from Staff and Committee (Study Chair and picture of Tower Bridge) and Music Centre from Missionaries.

Apart from visits to Yorkshire and later to Birmingham my diary is strangely blank, but we were still responsible for two Funds and for the Holiday Homes. Much was to follow.

Chapter 14

Rodborough

As we began to enjoy Rodborough and its garden, the delightful thing about our retirement was that we could be together for most of the time. Edith began to play the American Organ for the women's meeting at the Chapel in the village, and I had to be at H.Q. from time to time but often we were together when we called there on our way to and from Felixstowe and Overstrand. We were often at Walmer, taking Retired Missionaries and their wives to cater or to enjoy the holiday.

Preaching continued in a new area: Kemsing (6 services), Speldhurst Chapel (6), Staines (2), Five Oak Green, Hildenborough P. B. (5), Honor Oak (2), Forest Gate, London, Bells Yew Green (3), Vine Hall, Sevenoaks, Langton Parish Church (1), Waltham Abbey (2). We had 5 days at Arthog in the spring and longer in the autumn and called in at Birmingham. A visit to Yorkshire, staff at Felixstowe for Easter kept us busy. Another Parkinson's tour to Wales in July when we left our car with Doris Green, staying overnight to meet the party in London on the Saturday morning. We had got to know that area well.

A Miss Pisani, retired hospital matron, called on us one day and that led to us having Bible Study meeting in their flat in Ferbies Close, Speldhurst. There is a note about the Women's Meeting in December. Evidently the leader gave up and left Edith a note to close it! We got the little church meeting to agree to our joint leadership—Edith playing and taking over as she could. It went well for five years but involved us leaving for long runs to homes on a Tuesday morning. Looking back on the 7 years as District Secretary I noted that I had given addresses in 200 places, and as I went to many annually for Box-opening, Annual Meetings and to preach several times it mounted up to quite a total.

When Miss Pisani died I took the funeral and we continued to meet with her friend Miss Little until she moved.

Soon after coming to Rodborough Mr & Mrs Holmans called on us; they had recently moved from Langton Green with Marjorie their daughter. They proved to be very dear friends and Mr Holmans helped me erect the greenhouse. During the periods when we were away at homes he looked after it and kept an eye on the house. He came to the bakers most days and came for a chat, sitting in the kitchen.

1977

We spent some time at Westwood with Mr & Mrs Kaye, Clarie was in Cliff with me and he and I did some decorating while the ladies attended to other work.

We had a weekend with Jessie Lynn, and at the end of March again went to Arthog to get it ready for the season. It was quite a run (285 miles). Easter at Martello Place again, and further opportunities to preach. Ron Gurnett and his brother Joe were boys in Peckham when I went there, joined the church and went on with the Lord. Ron married Kath Dootson, a Rye Lane girl who brought many from high school to the Mission; they invited us to their home and arranged for me to preach at Plumstead Free Church, a strong fellowship. Later I took a series of midweek addresses as the church reviewed its ministry. April brought a new challenge—a large house in Crieff, Perthshire, had come to the Mission as a part legacy. We stayed in a small flat arranged by Mr Barr, our Scottish accountant, for a few nights until we got the place aired. We found it was like Arthog in that it was just as the owner had left it on going into hospital.

We were in Crieff from April 26 to May 6th for there was much to do. Crieff is a small town and we found it difficult to get furniture etc. Mr Barr and a friend brought a van load from London. We called at Starbeck on the way and there is a note '1093m on return'. We had little time to see the delightful district on that occasion. Then the usual visit to Overstrand, Martello Place, Walmer, St Leonards etc. In July we took another Parkinson's party to Llandudno, North Wales and were able to arrange a day trip to Bodnant Gardens, a famous beauty spot. Several local friends including Marjorie went with us and it was a happy week.

Martin and Ruth[1] came to stay for a few days. Was that the occasion when British Rail let them down? I waited at South Croydon, kept phoning Edith and then they appeared from the south instead of the north. Martin had sorted out the trains. Then was it the sad occasion when we took them home and as we drew up outside the house the pet white rabbit was being killed by a dog! It seemed so weird that we should go so far and appear just at that moment.

September brought another Parkinson's tour, this time to Scotland. Staying at Largs on the Ayrshire coast, we had day trips across Loch Lomond, to the Trossachs, Loch Katrine etc. Coach not too good and it broke down miles away from

[1] The grandchildren. Ruth was born in October 1964 and Martin in 1966. Judith, the third grandchild, was born in 1979.

Carlisle where we were due for lunch. I found we were being delayed at repairers for the lack of money, paid the £50 and we got on our way home. Refunded later.

In October we visited Babs, Hilda, May etc. in Yorkshire. Then to Arthog where the family joined us for a few happy days.

Westwood was broken into at the year end. We had locks on windows etc., but one was broken and the Grandfather clock was the only item the burglars could get out of the lounge window. Later I found a snapshot taken by Mr Andrews. (I had had photo's taken but the photographer had failed to take the clock.) With this snap we got about £600+ insurance. I noted 15,000 miles in the year.

Collected new car. Old had done 30269m, Jan. 7th.

In March we went to Starbeck and to Pilmoor each day, Tuesday to Thursday.

April to Arthog via Stow on the Wold. Home at the end of the week via Birmingham. End of April a new responsibility in Keswick. the L.C.M had had the use of the frontage of a house near the Convention Tent (in common with other Societies) representing the work. Now the lady was leaving and offered the house to the Mission at a reasonable price. Her son did not agree and he stripped it; even light bulbs. It was in a bad state and we had to start from scratch. We called in on our way to Crieff via Starbeck (571m) It seems we got the house ready then went to collect Sheila Macdonald from Edinburgh for the weekend. Went to Loch Erne, Loch Tay, Loch Fruchie then called in Keswick on the way home.

On May 16th there is an important note: 'IT'S A GIRL'—Judith, a third grandchild. The usual round, Overstrand, Martello Place, Westwood, St Leonards.

June 6th to make an attack on the Keswick problems. Mr Barr to bring a load of furniture, van broke down and they arrived in the night. Ten days hard work and was this the occasion when Edith went to the laundrette and a girl offered to help her and 'helped herself' to Edith's engagement ring and her ruby wedding ring? Once again Edith took this in her stride, but it was a sad day for both of us.

July 1 to Llandudno again for the week. Much appreciated the godly man in charge. A good party and trip, for a week. Hilda visited us as she usually did each year. August 24 to Sept. 1st 'children with us'. That was a joy to us both.

Sept. 30th to Eastbourne to 'give away' Eileen Devenish to Archie Barton mentioned previously. I note 31 opportunities to give addresses plus monthly Devotional at The Elms.

In October we did the usual clearance of the cottage bedding to Westwood, this had to be reversed in the Spring each year. At the end of the month to Arthog via Birmingham, stayed ten days. To Birmingham ready for the Baptism of Ruth and Martin on Nov. 5th. then home after the evening service.

To Yorkshire Starbeck Staithes, Pilmoor and preach Sunday evening.

To Birmingham for Christmas. Preached at Crowborough, the first of many occasions.

1979

The year began as usual with getting out holiday lists for staff. I had been able to offer vacant places, first to retired, then to office staff and then to staff of Edinburgh and other City Missions.

In March we had the day in Clapham and preached in the Baptist Church that made us welcome when we went to London in 1936. A key to our being accepted in another Baptist Church: Rye Lane Peckham.

A visit to Tilbury where T. Kappers ministered to foreign seamen.

March 31st to Stow, Gloucester, and Arthog to get it ready until 7th. Apr.

May 1st to Keswick, 3rd to Crieff, 12th Starbeck. Preach, home afterwards. 15th. Martello Pl., Sunny Corner, H.Q. to interview possible gardener, Mr Austin—a godly man. Still in touch (1994).

July 7/14 another Parkinson's Fellowship Tours to Llandudno, N. Wales. Good. We had brief devotional periods each evening with a brief message.

July 23rd: The episode mentioned earlier took place when Martin had to re-plan the train journey to Croydon South.

In August we used the garden for a Garden Party for the Women's Fellowship. I had an allotment alongside Mr Holman's.

Aug. 25th: We accepted a proffered holiday from a wealthy supporter I had met and went to Newquay in the West Country, our first visit to the area. Accommodation new but poor, double bed but one chair, shower etc. The 'Christian' party proved to be a bit snooty and we got away as much as possible, to Lands End, Falmouth etc.

Later we took another Parkinsons Tour to Torquay, Sheila Macdonald joined us. We were impressed with the miniature 'village' tiny church with music, little lawns etc. 41 Seater coach had difficulty with Dartmoor lanes but it went quite well though food was poor.

At this time there is a note 'Edith to Doctor': the beginning of less good health! Oct. 24 to Nov. 3rd Arthog. It was half term—did family join us? Yes!

In November we went to Yorkshire and had clutch trouble, dating from a car load stopped on the way up Cader Idris mountain. Starting no doubt damaged the clutch. When I asked the foreman if it would get me to London (garage in Harrogate) he said in true Yorkshire humour, "Well it's down hill all the way!" I had it renewed! Christmas at Birmingham.

1980

Early in the year Miss Sealey next door to our Peckham home died and left us a small legacy as did her sister. An interesting commentary on our life there as after about ten years we were able to minister to the whole family.

The usual spring time getting Homes ready, Arthog March 25/30 then to Pilmoor to look after my father as Norman was not well, Dorothy his daughter had looked after Pa; then Norman joined them, now they needed help. We went on April 3rd. Pa was alert and had a joke at my expense. I took his denture to clean and he thought I was a long time and said to Edith, "has he gone to London for them?" On April 17 he passed peacefully away and we returned home. Back to Pilmoor for funeral Sunday April 20th.

24th to Keswick etc.

May 17 another Parkinsons Tour, this time to Carbis Bay, a delightful house near St Ives, Cornwall. A good driver and a happy party. Lands End, Newquay, Penzance, Falmouth etc.

Hilda with us in June. The usual trips to homes all season.

I was pleased to be asked again to speak at the Civil Service C. U. in London, having done some days with them at their retreat earlier.

To Yorkshire Aug. 23rd then on to Crieff August 28th. to Sept. 5. This time we did see a bit more of the district.

All this time we kept in close touch with the Old People's home—Committee etc.

Closed down homes in the Autumn, Arthog Oct. 22 to 29 then on to Keswick and back via Birmingham.

Christmas in Birmingham again.

One year I checked and we had slept away from home on 70 nights doing Homes work.

1981

The usual round of Spring activity getting homes ready for the season. Easter at Martello Place, May to Keswick. This house—or rather half house; it had no back door—was the most trouble and least satisfactory of the four homes we opened up. The district is of course delightful, but I did not have liberty in conducting the necessary work there, although I had contacted a Trust and been granted £2000 towards it. For some reason we had to make a second visit that Spring and went there from Overstrand. Another visit to Yorkshire.

June 6th another visit to Carbis Bay with Parkinsons Tours, once again a very happy time of fellowship in a good area. Lands End, Newquay, Truro, Falmouth etc.

July 4th to 11th another Parkinsons Tour, this time to Scarborough, a new one for us. Our bedroom was in the attic and we had a thunderstorm so got a not very pleasant view of the sky. It was not ideal but again a good area; we went to Coastal towns and had a day at Castle Howard, and a day in York when Hilda joined us. David came to stay later in July.

To Crieff early in October with time to travel around a bit. Then for the weekend to Edinburgh to be with Sheila Macdonald and home via Pilmoor, etc.

October 22nd to Arthog. David came by train to the halt having told the guard that he wished to alight we met him there and Maureen and the children joined us for half term later. We closed the house for the winter and left for Keswick on 31st. A delightful run by the lake and Bala where the girl from south of Arthog walked for her Bible so many years ago. (Mary Jones.)

The district south of Keswick was a lovely picture with beech leaves turning to their autumn colours. We enjoyed this last visit to Keswick where we had spent the first days of our married life.

On November 19th. we went to Sunny Corner, Overstrand for the bedding, and to Martello Place. On Nov. 23rd I went to the Committee of the L.C.M to be thanked and to hand over the keys to Mr Gordon Holland the new Holiday Homes Secretary. We had covered the homes for 9 seasons completely and had opened up St Leonards, Arthog, Crieff, and Keswick homes. It was time to give up for Edith found it all very tiring, and it was time for me too.

To Birmingham for Christmas.

1982

The year began with Edith going into Tonbridge Cottage Hospital for a prolapse operation. It was not urgent but Dr. Hoare thought it might help her. She had quite a lot of visitors.

David and family were with us for Easter, and I collected Mr & Mrs Kaye from Herstmonceux for the day, in May. They like us had moved into a bungalow left to the Mission. I had met the donor when preaching.

Later in May we visited Yorkshire again and I preached at Starbeck, reminding them that I had started in Feb. 1932 as their Missioner. Hilda visited us, we probably brought her back.

In July we took a Parkinsons Tour party to Scarborough, Yorkshire again, to York, Whitby, Castle Howard etc. This was to be our last: they booked us for Llandudno the following year but we could not do it.

In September a friend of our Peckham days, Florrie Claydon died. I had been executor for her mother and then for her; as I was getting on I had suggested Ron Weston, one of our N. Peckham 'boys', join me. As we cleared the house he took home papers to sort and found that Florrie had nominated me to have her savings. This was a surprise, though I had a dim recollection that she had said years ago that she wanted me to have them and I had said, "no, use the money yourself!" It was, for us, quite a considerable sum, that has made life easier.

To the annual Trustees Meeting of the Overcomer Trust— we had been friendly with J. C. Metcalfe from Starbeck Days and he often stayed in our home.

October saw us at Arthog again, and David and family joined us there.

I was found to have glaucoma and went to a specialist—daily drops for the rest of my life.

1983

Early in the year we were back in Peckham for preaching at Rye Lane Chapel, stayed with Ken Daniel and his wife.

Mr and Mrs Lyall were in the village; Mrs Lyall was a very dear friend to us both. Ex China Inland Mission folk.

On July 11th. we went to Starbeck, ready for the celebration of our Golden Wedding. The Mission ladies gladly agreed to cater for this and all our available family joined us for that very happy occasion. This was an occasion for profound thanksgiving for us both, and it seems a suitable time to bring this record to an end, except to mention that my brother Norman died on Oct. 14th and I was not well enough to go to the funeral—David went instead. Then Edith's sister May died April 2nd. 1985.

Perhaps I ought to add some of the outstanding items from following years.

A special joy to us both was that we were well enough to take part in the Centenary of the Starbeck Mission in 1986. There is a brochure telling of the Mission from early days. Of special interest is the report that a Mr Prentice held a special mission in 1896. He would be the elderly City Missionary I met in 1936+ and his son followed him into the L.C.M

For many months a good deal of time was spent in appeals to Trusts for the funds to build a second wing at the rear of the Elms (Old People's Home) I had some help with letters but had to work through hundreds of Trust details in the £50+ Book. About £80,000 came in through this means and the Robert Speirs Wing was opened in 1988. Edith was far from well but able to be present. There is a thanksgiving report. God has been so good to us in so many ventures He has led into.

Then because the speaker booked was not well, I had the joy of addressing the 40th thanksgiving Day at The Elms.

Edith had been very disappointed that she was not well enough to attend the wedding of our granddaughter Ruth. Having struggled to get a new dress she came sadly to the conclusion that the effort was just too much. That was in August 1987, but she recovered enough to go to Birmingham for a celebration of the wedding of our grandson Martin who had married a lovely Dutch girl in Holland where they both worked for Operation Mobilisation.

As we were well into our 58th year of united witness she became aware that, like the apostle Paul, the time of her 'departure was at hand'. As we drove away from our son's home in Southampton that last Christmas she said, "I shall never come here again". I passed it off, but weakness increased until she said, "I'm only half alive." Then one sleepless night she 'saw' her long deceased brother and said "I'm coming". Such is the mystery of our earthbound life.

Then came the evening that having got her tucked up in bed I said, "what shall I read?" and she said "Psalm 23". So I read that beloved Psalm and then, for the first time in our married life, we sang together at the close of a day the chorus our young Christian folk in Peckham so loved:

Surely goodness and mercy shall follow me
All the days, all the days of my life,
And I shall dwell in the house of the Lord for ever.
And I shall feast at the table spread for me!
Surely goodness and mercy shall follow me
All the days of my life.

Soon after that she fell and I had to get a neighbour to help me lift her back into bed. The outcome was that our doctor, not being able to get her a bed in either of our local hospitals, suggested a local nursing home (within walking distance! Such is the loving care of our Lord.) to which she was admitted. Just one week later, and in great weakness, she turned to me and said, "ask Jesus to take me Home". A difficult prayer for me to pray. That was on the Monday evening and during Tuesday night, the prayer was answered. At the age of 81 she went to be 'with Christ' and so a lifetimes friendship, companionship and joint witness was ended. She had played the piano for our Mission Centres, accompanied me on Sunday preaching engagements and in a true Godly fashion had been my helper and co-operated with me in every path of our journey. And I miss her terribly. Psalm 16 verse 11 has been a great comfort to me. For her 'fullness of joy and pleasures for ever more'. For me 'the path of life' made plain.

Epilogue

After my mother's death, my father continued to live at Rodborough, being well able to look after himself. As the little Baptist church had only a Sunday morning service, he went to the parish church on Sunday evenings and was eventually accepted as part of the church leadership. It was characteristic that his funeral was held in the parish church and conducted by the Baptist Pastor.

For a short period at the end of his life he went into a home, Cornford House, Pembury, run by the Overseas Missionary Fellowship, and died there of bladder cancer on July 30, 1998, at the age of 88.

The memory of the just is blessed.

Printed in Great Britain
by Amazon

19137624R00119